Praying the Word over your Wounds
Edition 2

SAM Morrison

Other Books, Journals and Devotionals by SAM Morrison:

Shining Light into the Darkness
Intentional Acts of Loving-Kindness
31 Days of Encouragement, 1 Day at a Time
A Year of Thankfulness
Legacy
A Year of Proverbs
Fuel your Body
Prayer Journal
A Pondering Place – The Original
A Pondering Place – Scripture Version
A Pondering Place – Business Version
A Pondering Place – Recovery Version
Sweet Baby

All Scriptures are from the Holy Bible,
English Standard Version (ESV)

Cover Photo credit: Robert H. Dunaway

ISBN-13:978-1717586360
ISBN-10:1717586368

Dedication:

This devotional is dedicated to all those that have suffered in the past. Life can hurt but the Word of God heals. Pray these scriptures over yourself and those you love. Write them on your heart and draw on them in your time of need. Reach out to God and feel the peace that only He can provide.

SAM

Contents:

40 Scriptures with a prayer for each one.

The prayers included are not "special". They are just written from the heart. Please feel free to add to or take away from the included prayers.

The important thing is to share your heart with God.

Be sure to take the time to journal your prayers and thoughts. Taking the time to do this will allow you to look back over time and see all that God has done for you and how you have healed from your past wounds.

Definitions:

Word
the Bible, or a part of it

Prayer
a solemn request or expression of thanks to God

Wound
an injury inflected on someone

Note from SAM:

Everyone has been wounded. It is part of life. How we deal with our wounds will determine if they bring glory to God. You may have made choices that have created your own wounds or have been wounded by someone. How you were wounded is not the issue, allowing yourself to heal from the wounds is. Once a wound heals it will turn into a scar. Do not be afraid to show your scars. They will give you a chance to tell the story of your healing that came from the one true God who created everything that was, is and will ever be.

Word:

For I consider that the sufferings of this present time are not worth comparing with the glory that is to be revealed to us. Romans 8:18

Prayer:

Father – I thank you now, even in this time of struggling, for loving me and protecting me. Please give me the strength that can only come from you to endure and continue to trust that you are working everything out for my good. I love you. Amen.

Word:

But you, O Lord, are a shield about me, my glory, and the lifter of my head. I cried aloud to the Lord, and he answered me from his holy hill.

Psalm 3:3-4

Prayer:

Lord – when I read this scripture I remember that you hear my prayers and that you are the lifter of my head. Thank you for being my shield and for answering my prayers. Please guide me today as I remember that you are my provider. I love you. Amen.

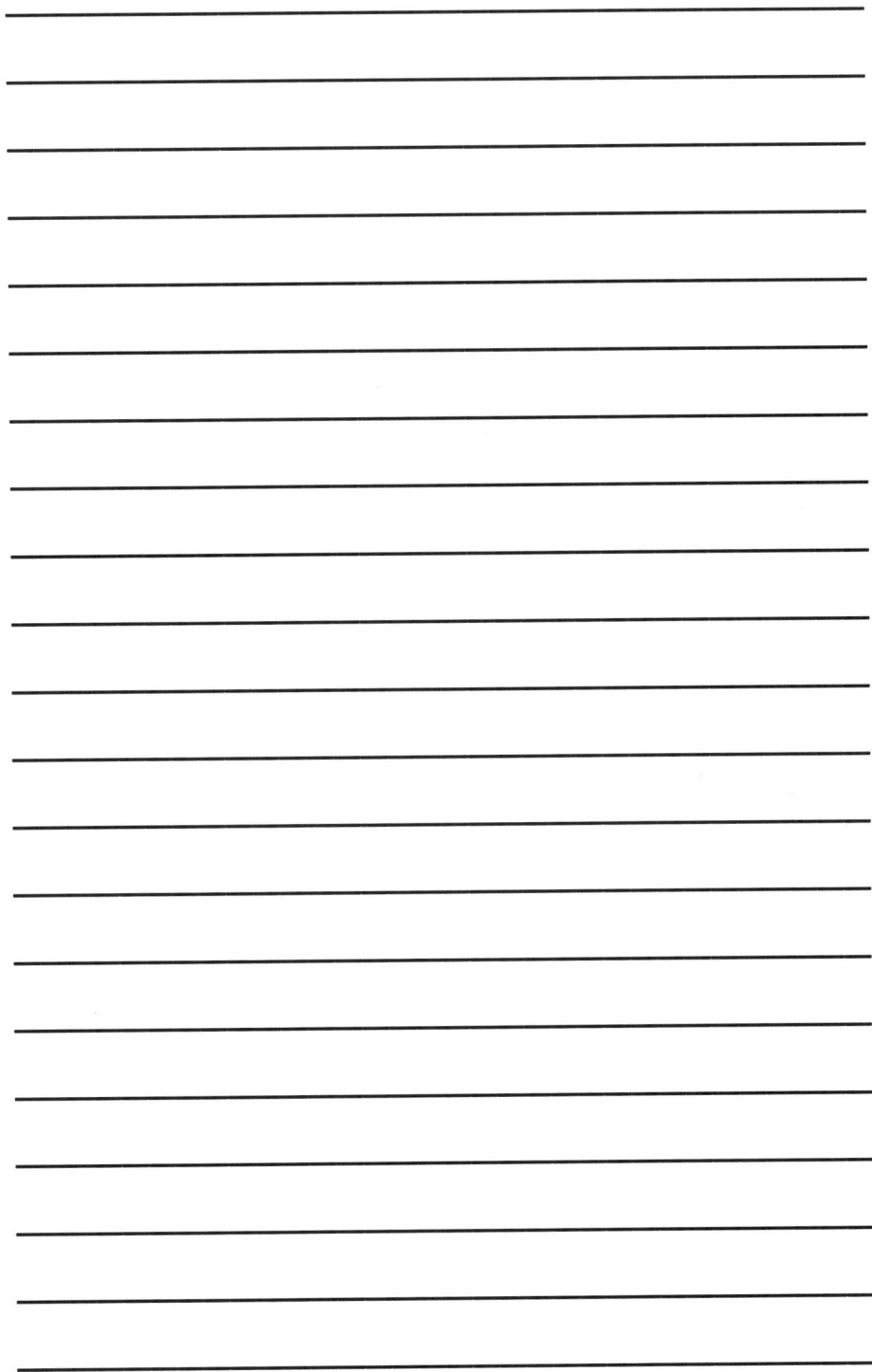

Word:

For I am convinced that neither death nor life, neither angels nor demons, neither the present nor the future, nor any powers, neither height nor depth, nor anything else in all creation, will be able to separate us from the love of God that is in Christ Jesus our Lord. Romans 8:38-39

Prayer:

Oh Father – what a wonderful thing it is to be your child. Thank you for saving me and making it so that nothing can separate me from you – ever. I love you. Amen.

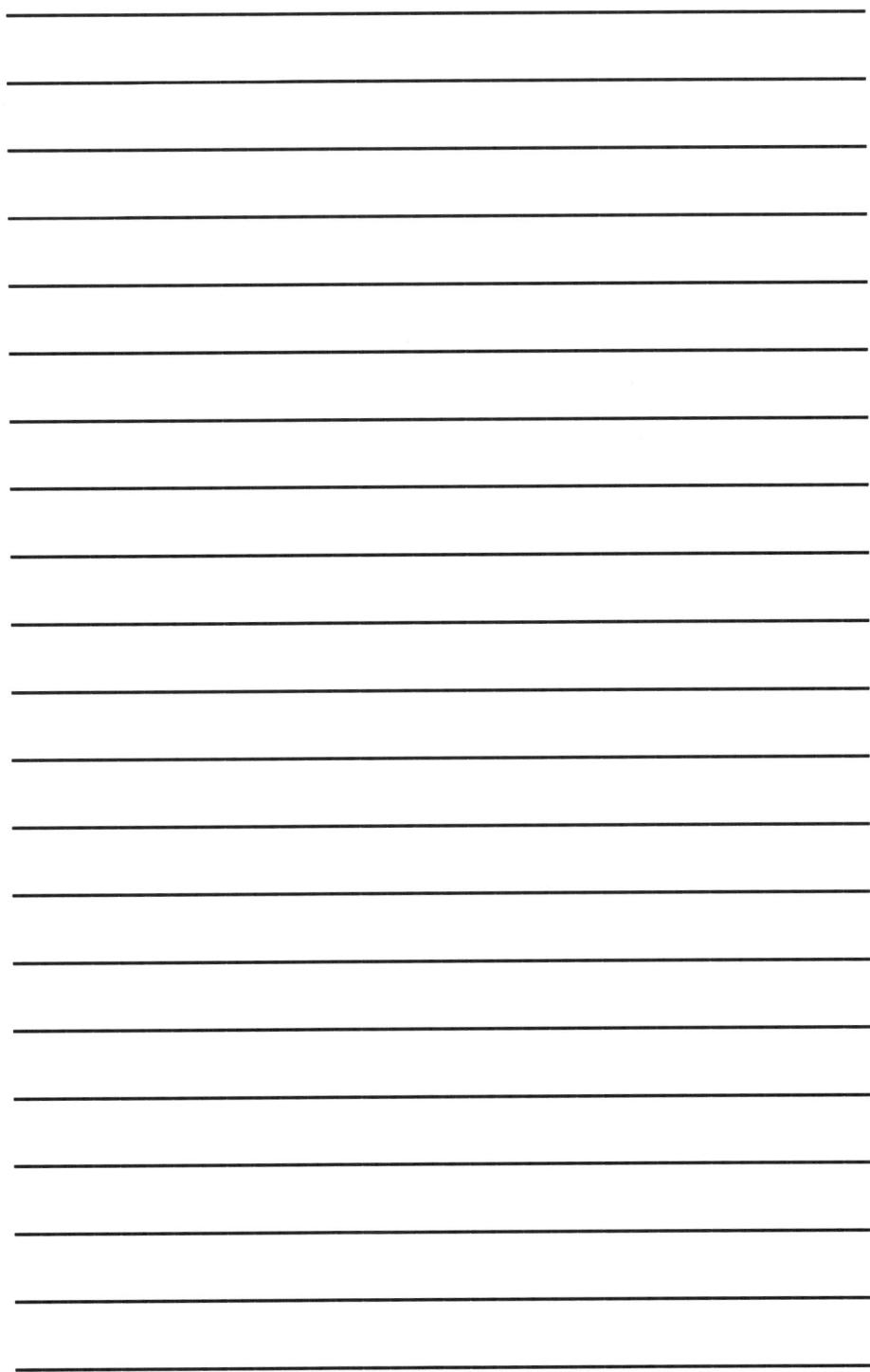

Word:

But by the grace of God I am what I am, and his grace toward me was not in vain. On the contrary, I worked harder than any of them, though it was not I, but the grace of God that is with me.
1 Corinthians 15:10

Prayer:

Father – today I ask that you remind me that everything I am and have is yours. All the glory goes to you and you alone. Help me live my life for you and shine your light bright today and every day. I love you. Amen.

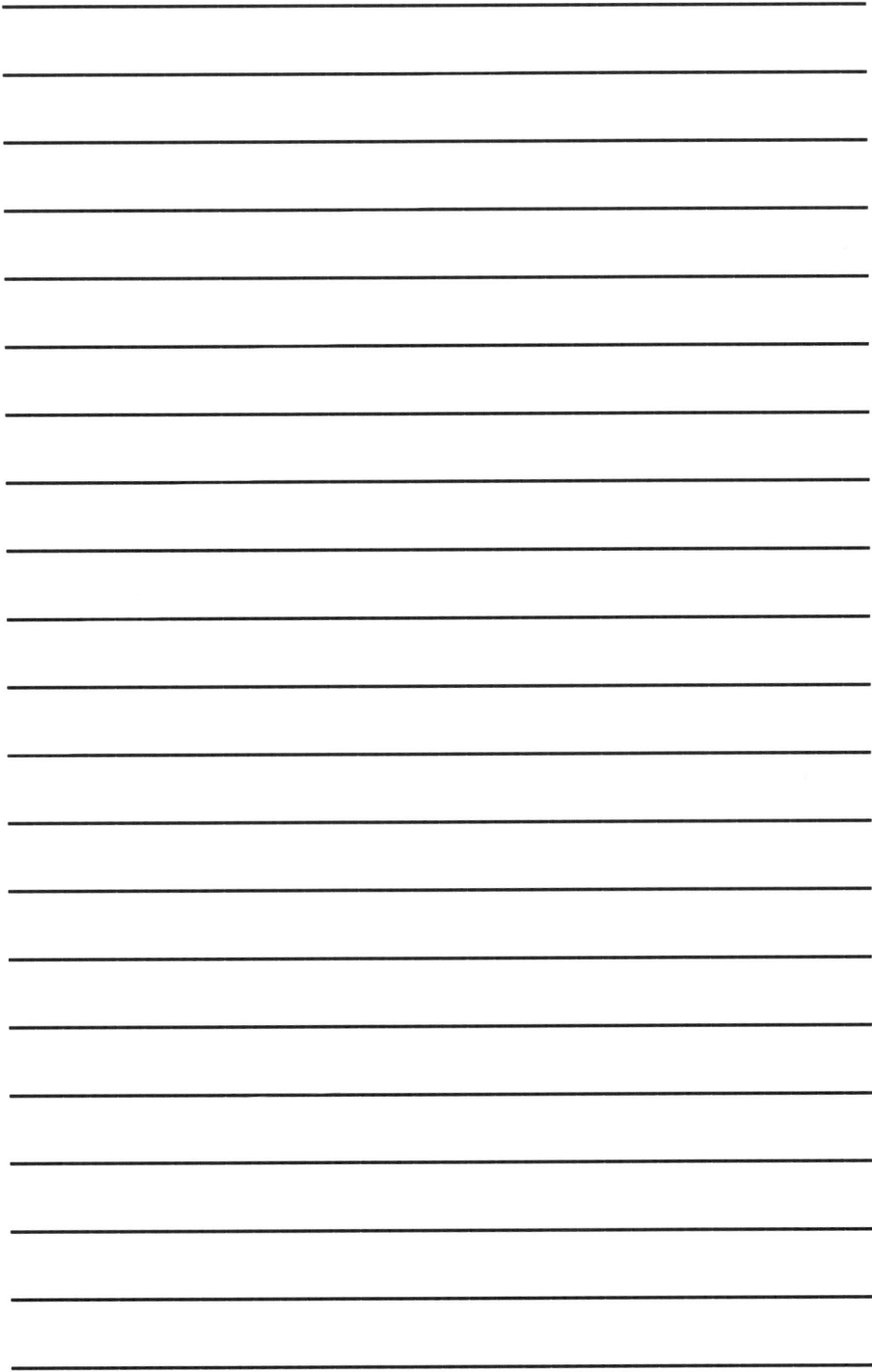

Word:

You, dear children, are from God and have overcome them, because the one who is in you is greater than the one who is in the world. 1 John 4:4

Prayer:

Papa – GREATER – you are greater than the one in the world. You are greater than the thing that tried to destroy me and make me feel unqualified to be your child. Thank you for loving me and calling me your child. I trust you.
Amen.

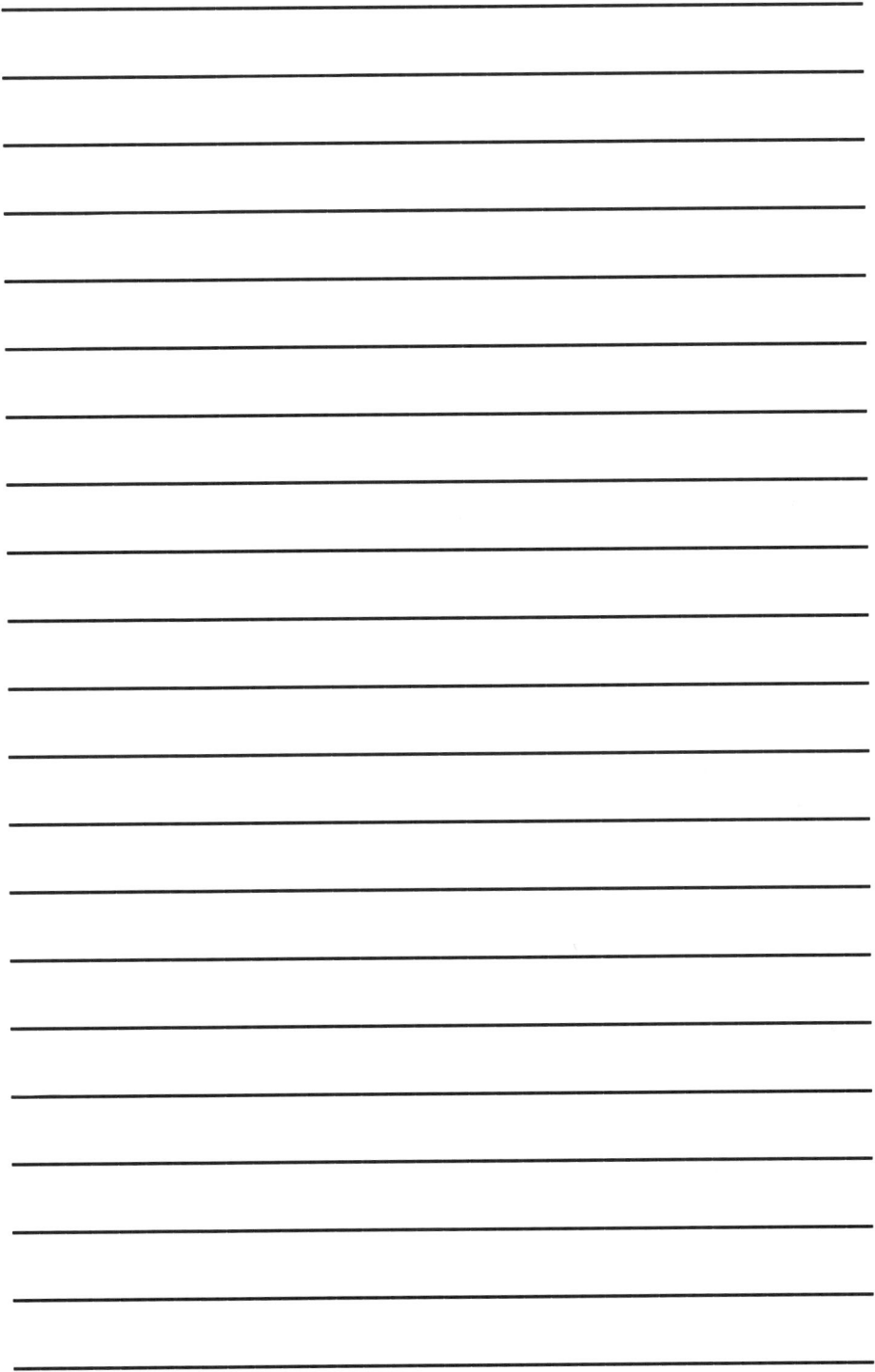

Word:

Who comforts us in all our troubles, so that we can comfort those in any trouble with the comfort we ourselves receive from God. For just as we share abundantly in the sufferings of Christ, so also our comfort abounds through Christ. 2 Corinthians 1:4-5

Prayer:

Abba – some days are just hard. Thank you for being my comfort in time of need. Because of you I really can face tomorrow. I love you. Amen.

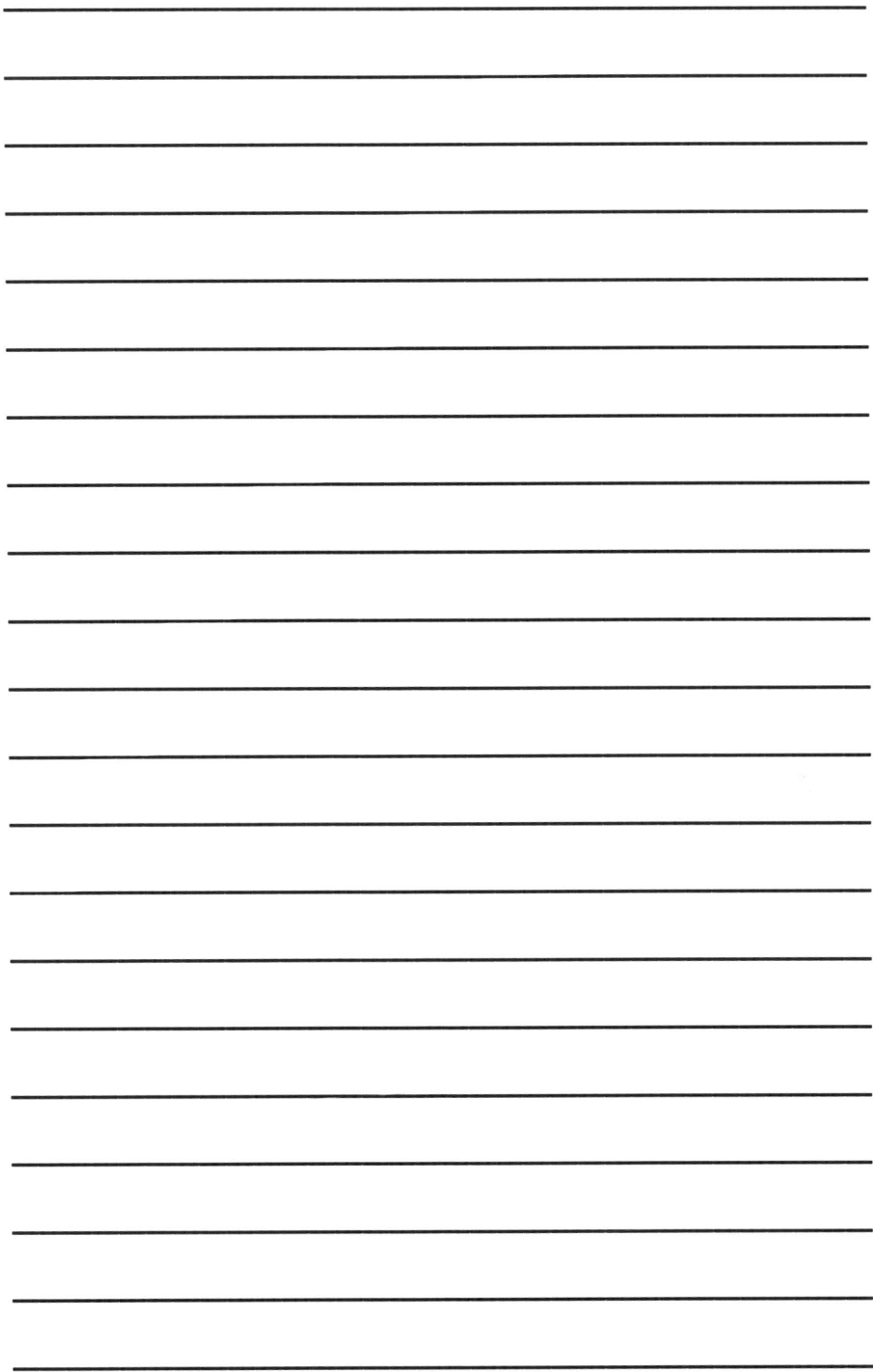

Word:

Be still and know that I am God. I will be exalted among the nations, I will be exalted in the earth! Psalm 46:10

Prayer:

Father – today I want to just stop and be still and let you love me in a way that I sometimes forget to do. Hold me Lord and let me remember that you are God and you will be exalted in all the earth. Even when it seems like chaos and pain are winning I trust that you have everything in control. I love you. Amen.

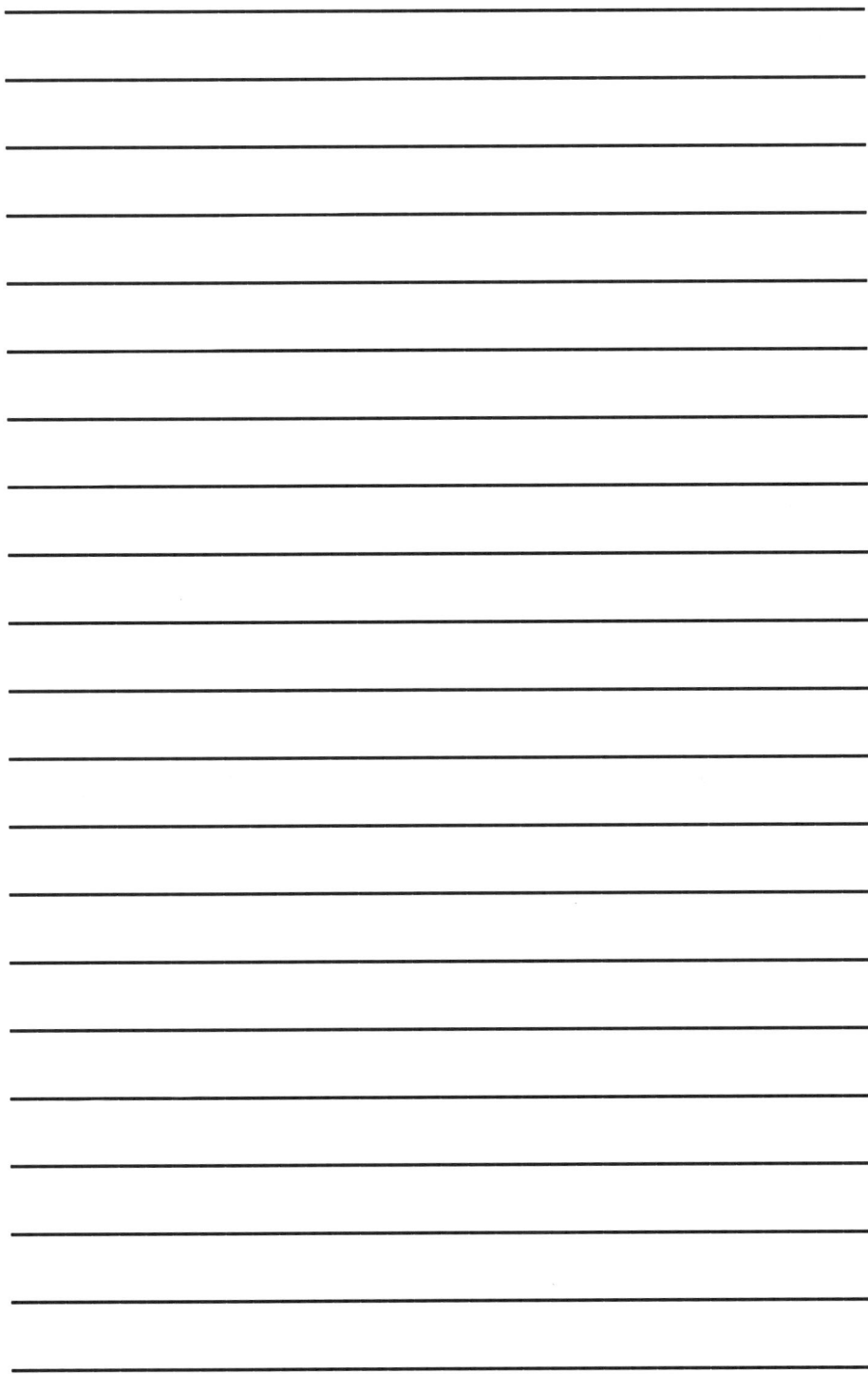

Word:

For God gave us a spirit not of fear but of power and love and self-control.
2 Timothy 1:7

Prayer:

Daddy – I love you. You gave me a spirit of power – love and self-control. Thank you. Please help me remember that even on the days where it feels like I have no power, no love, and no self-control because your word says you gave it to me – I have it. I am claiming that today and believe that your Word is true. I love you. Amen.

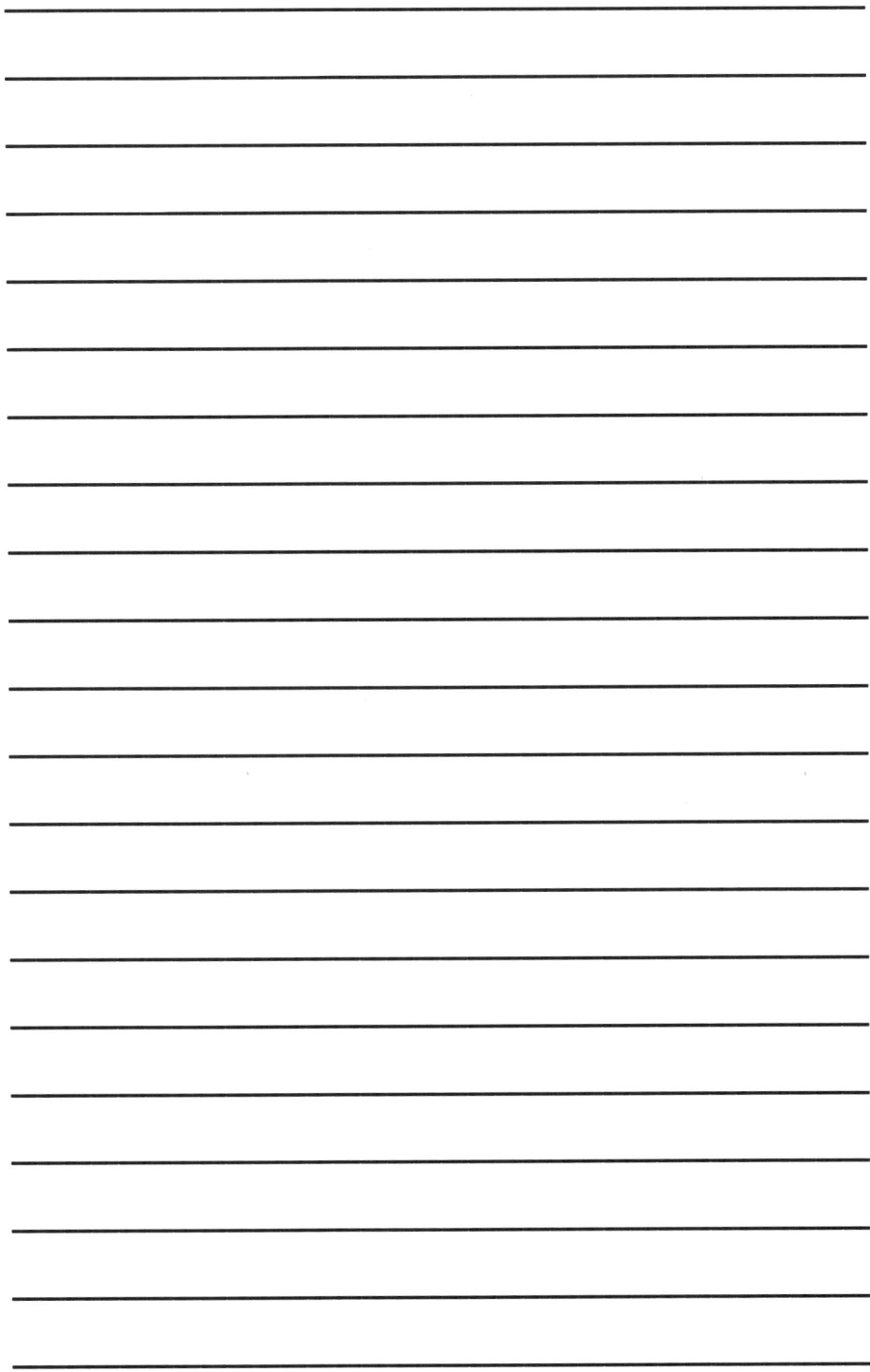

Word:

Now to him who is able to do far more abundantly than all that we ask or think, according to the power at work within us, to him be glory in the church and in Christ Jesus throughout all generations, forever and ever. Amen. Ephesians 3:20-21

Prayer:

Father – heal me from the inside out. I give you my mind, my body, my spirit. I want to give you my entire life and have you get all the glory for how you heal and work in me. I love you. Amen.

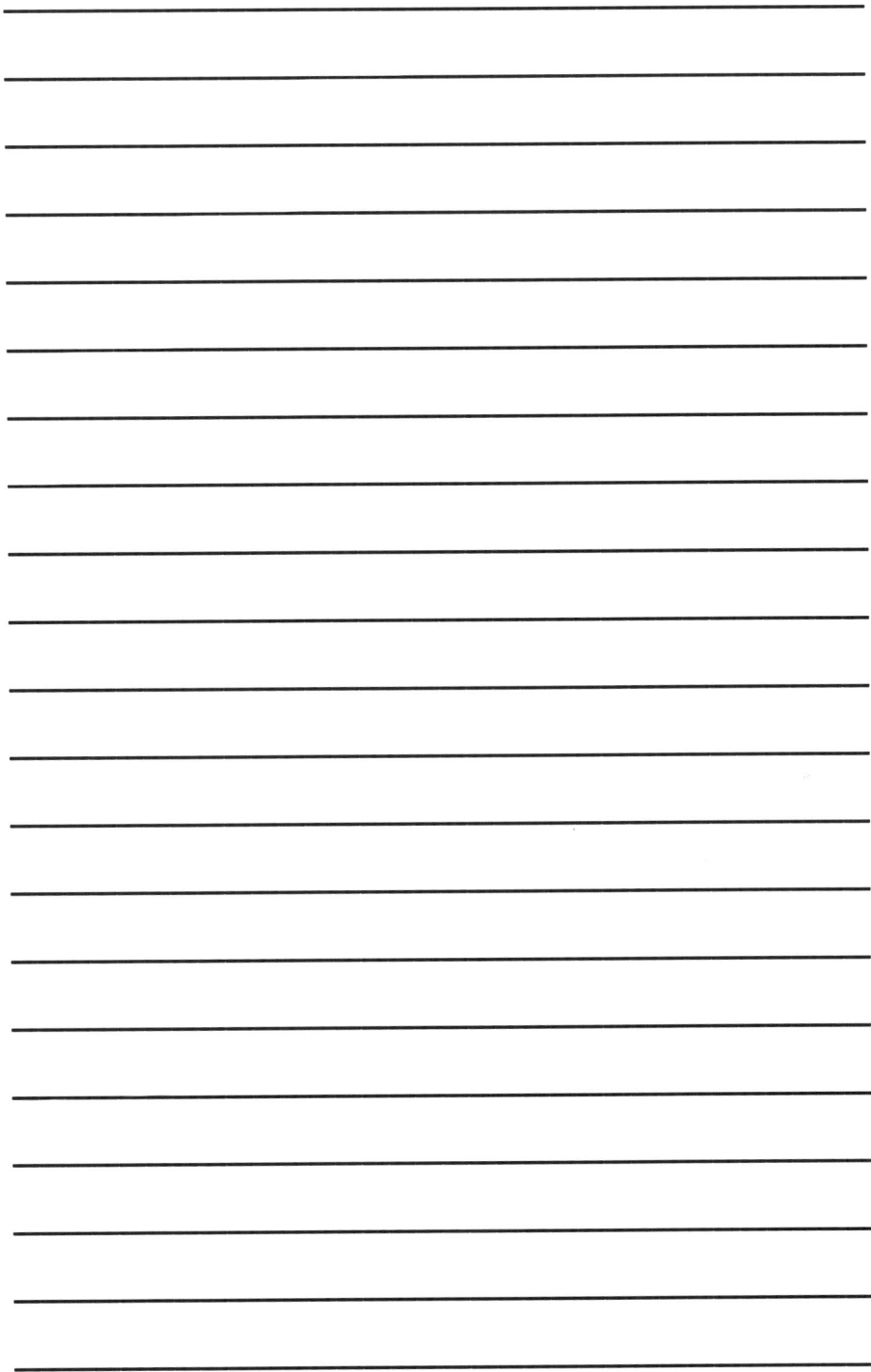

Word:

It is for freedom that Christ has set us free. Stand firm and do not let yourselves be burdened again by the yolk of slavery! Galatians 5:1

Prayer:

Papa – what a glorious day to be remembered. The day I was set free. Please help me stand firm and not ever go back to what bound me. The freedom I have in you is so sweet. Make me crave it ever more. I love you. Amen.

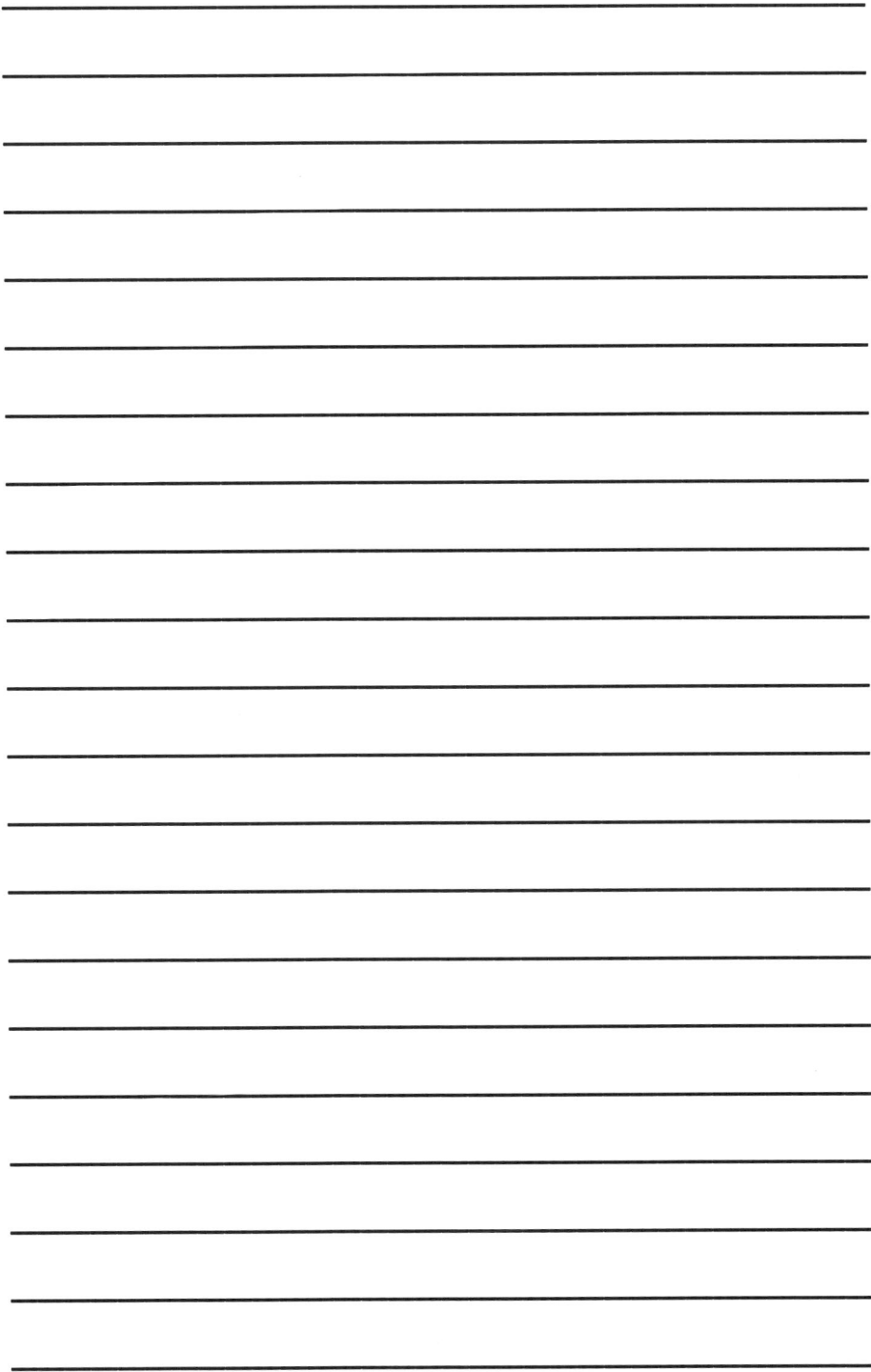

Word:

You intended to harm me, but God intended it for good to accomplish what is now being done, the saving of many lives. Genesis 50:20

Prayer:

Daddy – thank you for turning what was meant to harm me into something good. My life is different because of what you are creating in and through me. The mess of my life really can be my message to the world because of how you make everything beautiful. Thankfully Yours. Amen.

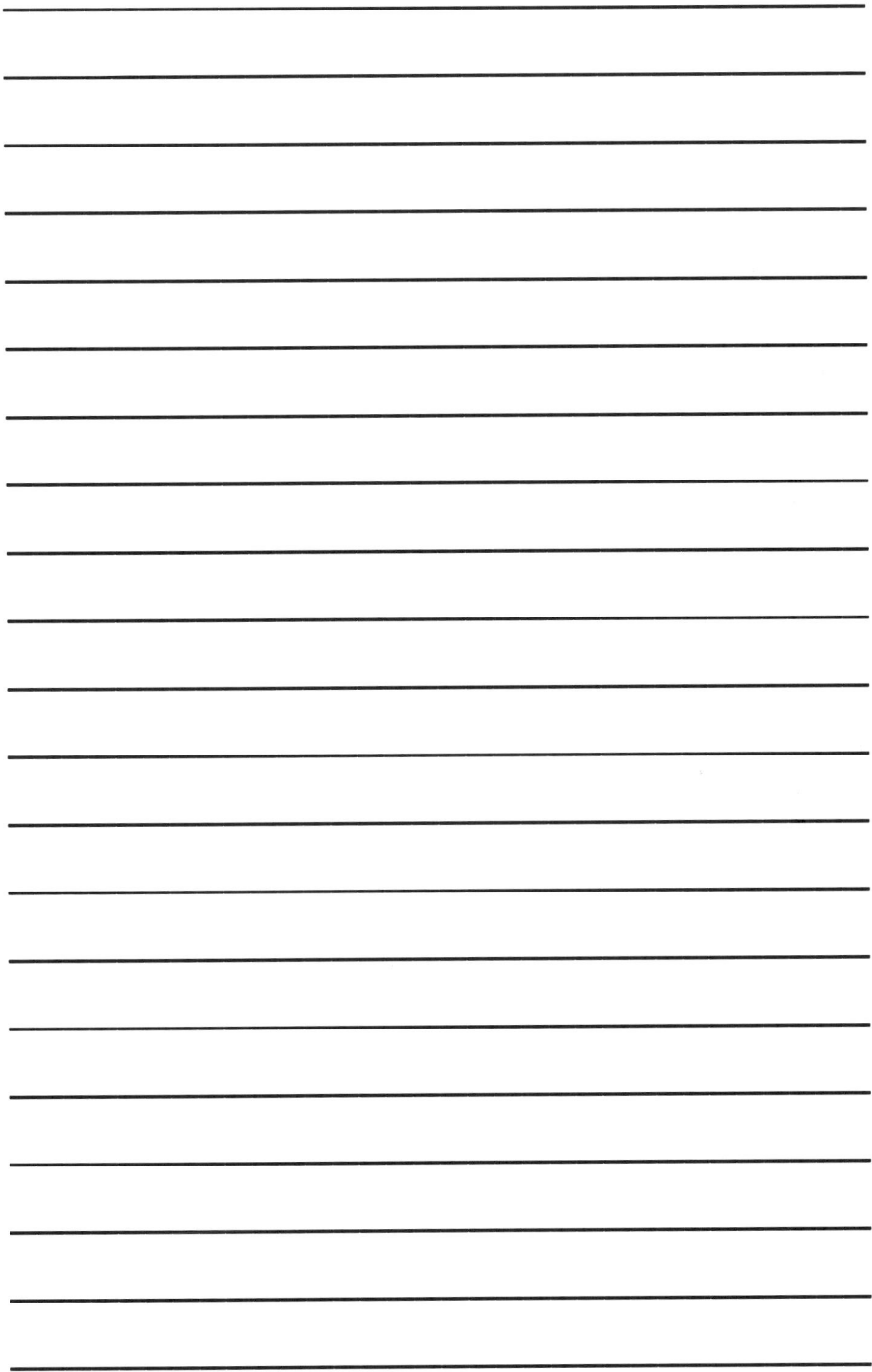

Word:
Faith is being certain of what we hope for and sure of what we do not see.
Hebrews 11:1

Prayer:
Father – some days I just can't "see it". I can't see how you are healing me a little more each day. But because I believe your word is true and trust that you love me I have the faith I need. But oh Lord – on the days when it is hard, please give me more faith. I know you will never leave me. Help me believe it even more on the hard days. I love you.
Amen.

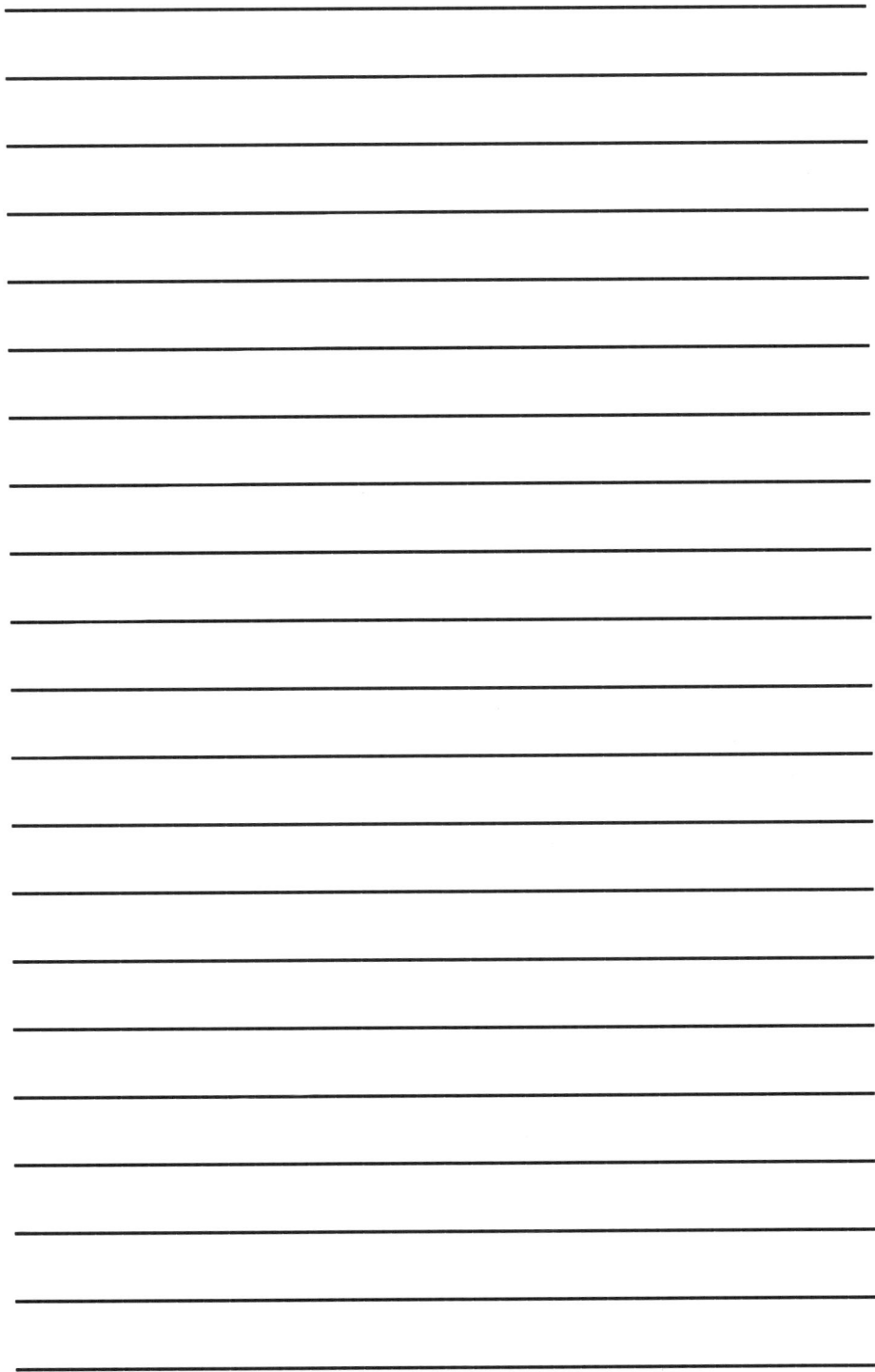

Word:
For I know the plans I have for you, declares the Lord, plans for welfare and not for evil, to give you a future and a hope. Jeremiah 29:11

Prayer:
Father – My prayer today is that not only do I know this verse, but I believe that it is true. May my actions reflect the fact that I know that you have a plan for my life and I am yours. Somehow it makes it easier to know that every hurt and tear will not be forgotten by you. It really is all working towards the plan you have for my life. I love you. Amen.

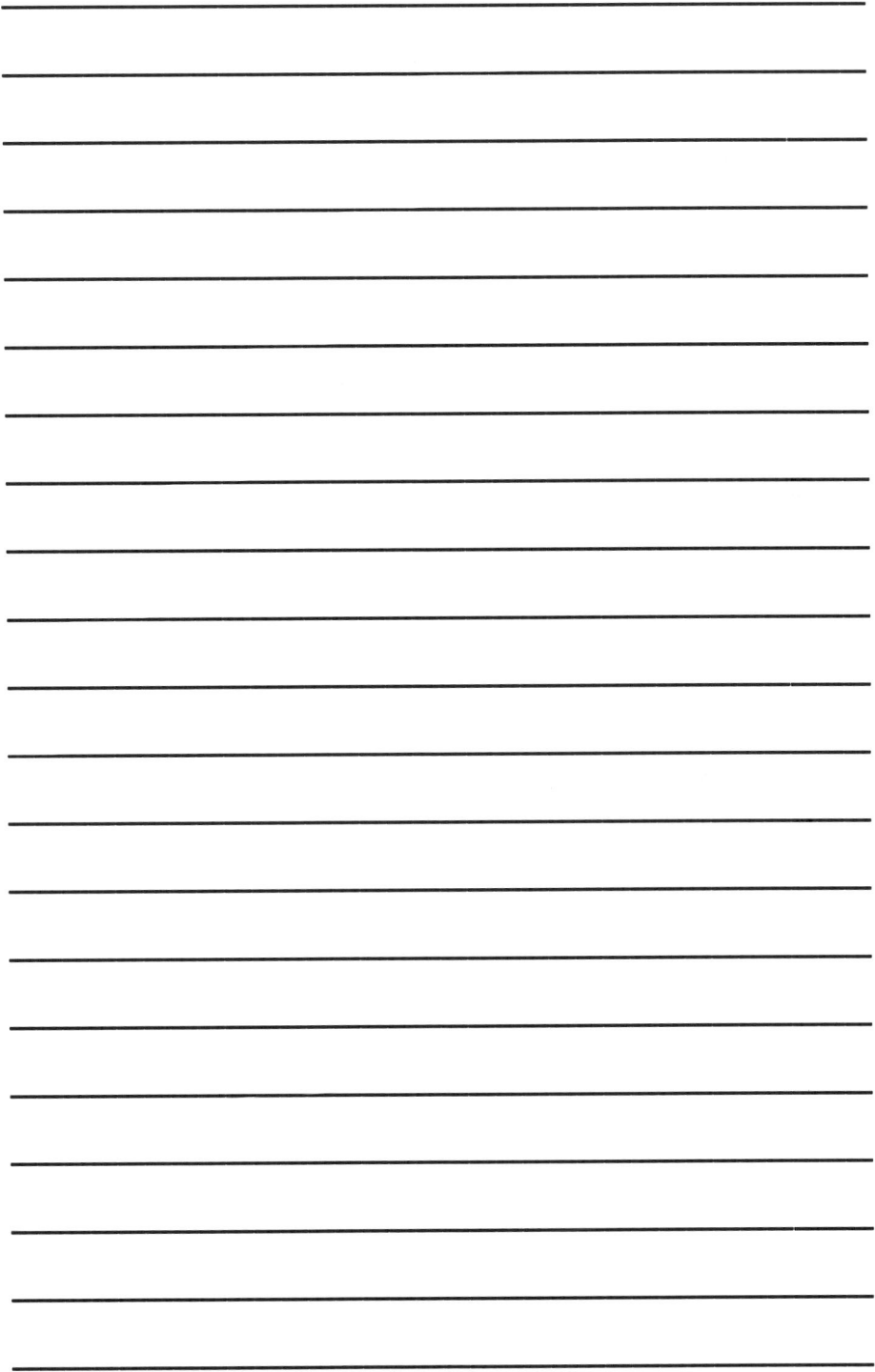

Word:

I am the door. If anyone enters by me, he will be saved and will go in and out and find pasture. The thief comes only to steal and kill and destroy. I came that they may have life and have it abundantly. John 10:9-10

Prayer:

Father – I believe your word. Thank you for coming to give me life and life to the full. Give me the strength to lean on you today and know that my hope comes from you. Nothing I have done or have had done to me can separate me from you. I am thankful for this truth. Amen.

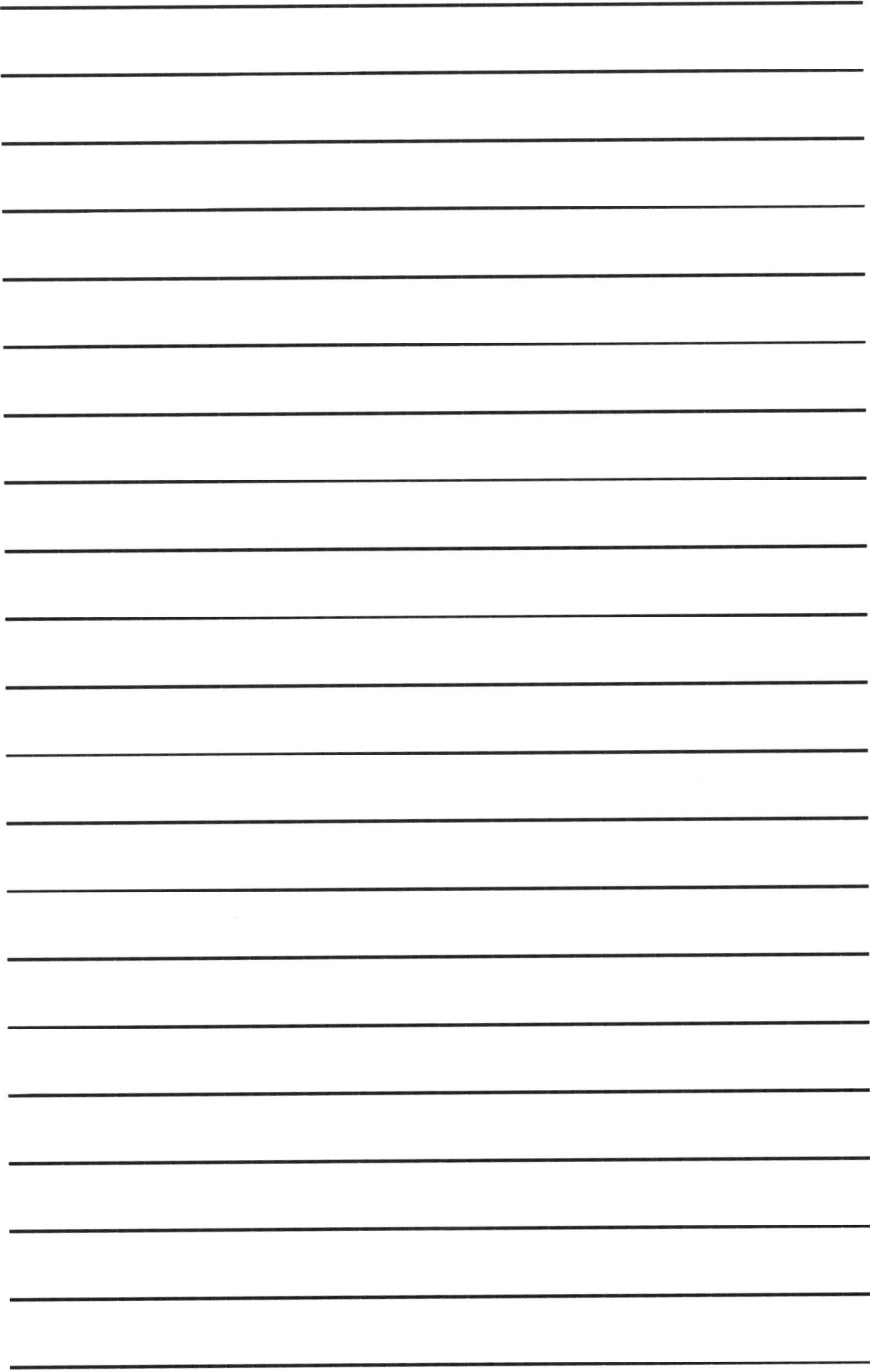

Word:

I have told you these things, so that in me you may have peace. In this world you will have trouble. But take heart! I have overcome the world. John 16:33

Prayer:

Abba – what great news this scripture brings me. You have overcome the world! With you by my side – even though I face struggles – I know how the story ends. LOVE WINS. Thank you for giving me peace for the struggles of today. I love you. Amen.

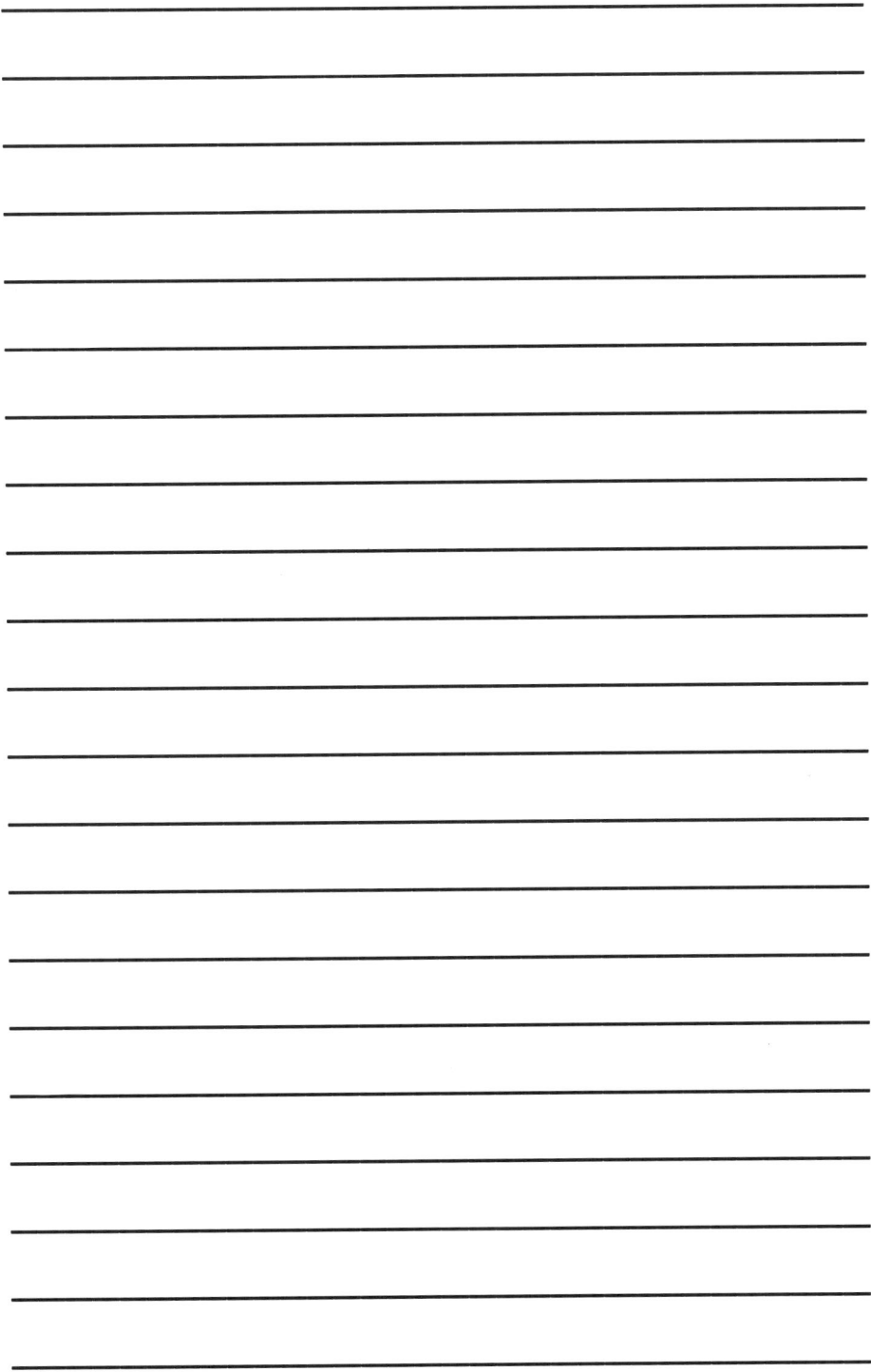

Word:
No man shall be able to stand before you all the days of your life. Just as I was with Moses, so I will be with you. I will not leave you or forsake you.
Joshua 1:5

Prayer:
Father – what a promise we have in this verse. You will never leave me or forsake me. I claim this promise today and believe that even though some days are challenging I can have courage because you are with me. You are my rock. You are my deliverer and no one or thing can ever change that.
Graciously Yours. Amen.

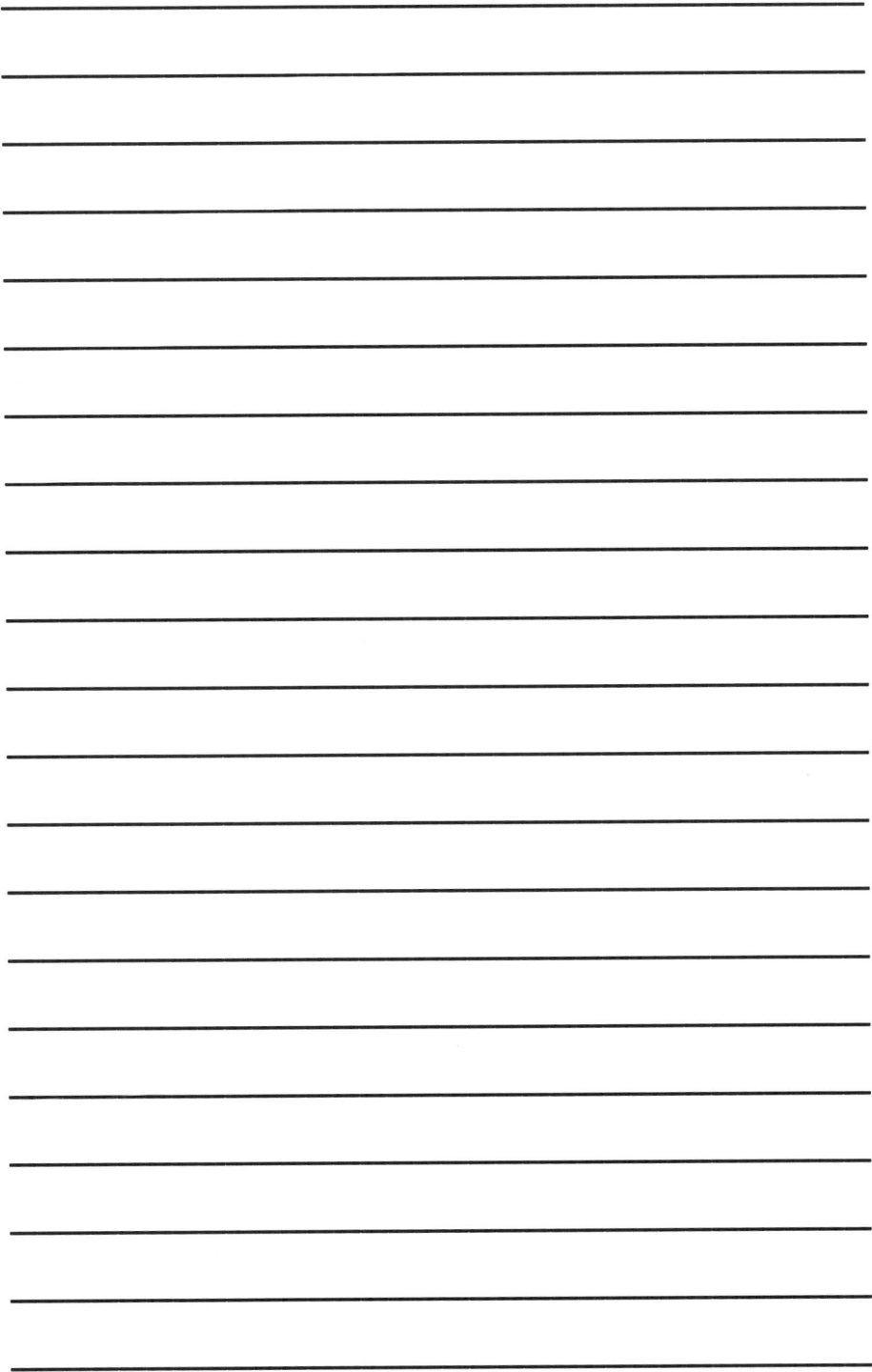

Word:

Have I not commanded you? Be strong and courageous. Do not be frightened, and do not be dismayed, for the Lord your God is with you wherever you go.
Joshua 1:9

Prayer:

Dear God – some days I feel frightened and not very strong. Please help me believe this verse is true. Help me walk in all the truth of your word and even when it does not feel like I am enough. Remind me that I am and that you will always be with me. I love you so much.
Amen.

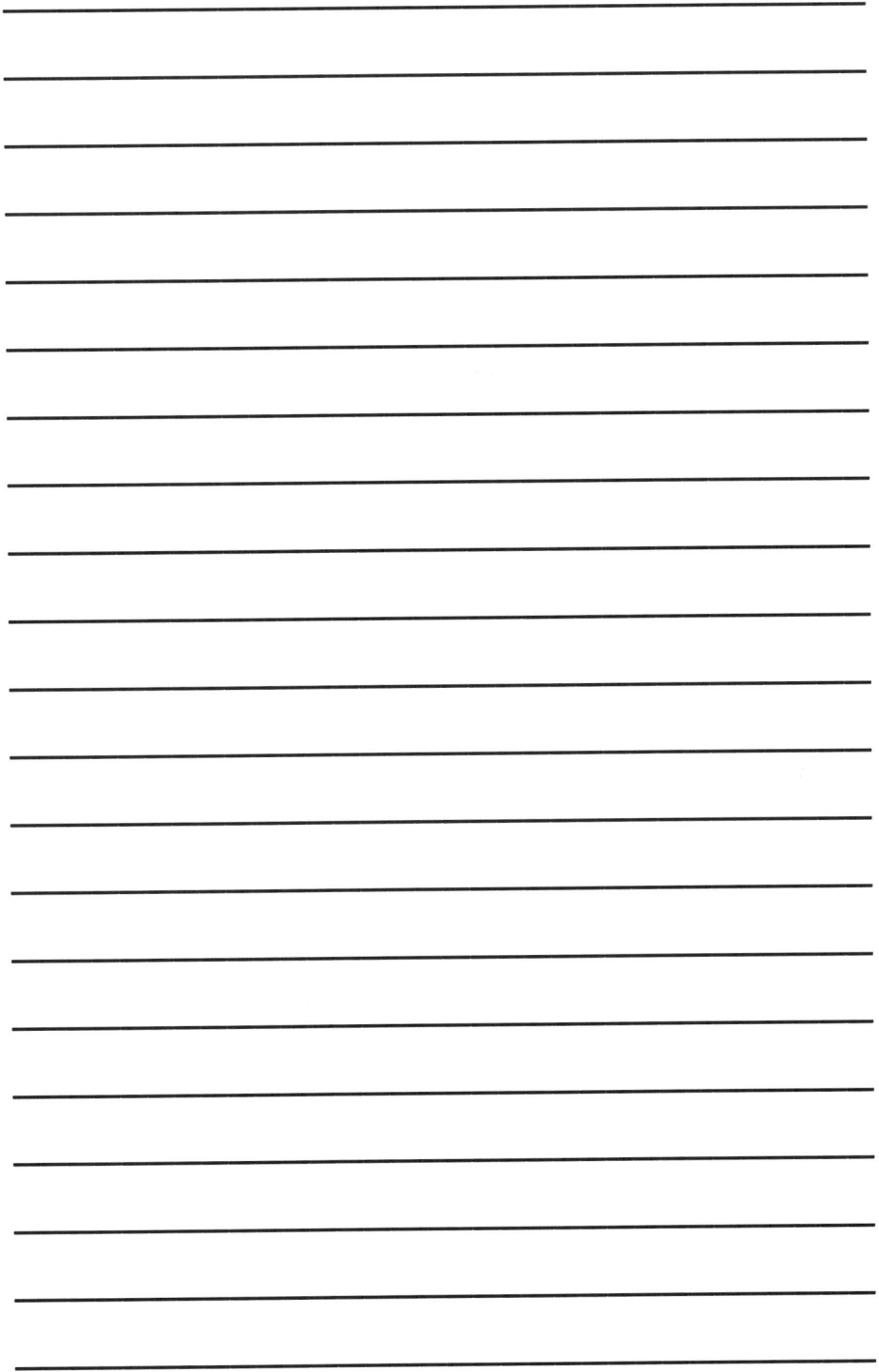

Word:

For what will it profit a man if he gains the whole world and forfeits his soul? Or what shall a man give in return for his soul? Matthew 16:26

Prayer:

Papa – please help me live in a way that connects my soul more to you every day. In my pain and sadness sometimes, I am prone to forget who I belong to. Please remind me today and every day that I am completely yours. Let me live my life for you and shine the light of your love everywhere I go. Forever yours. Amen.

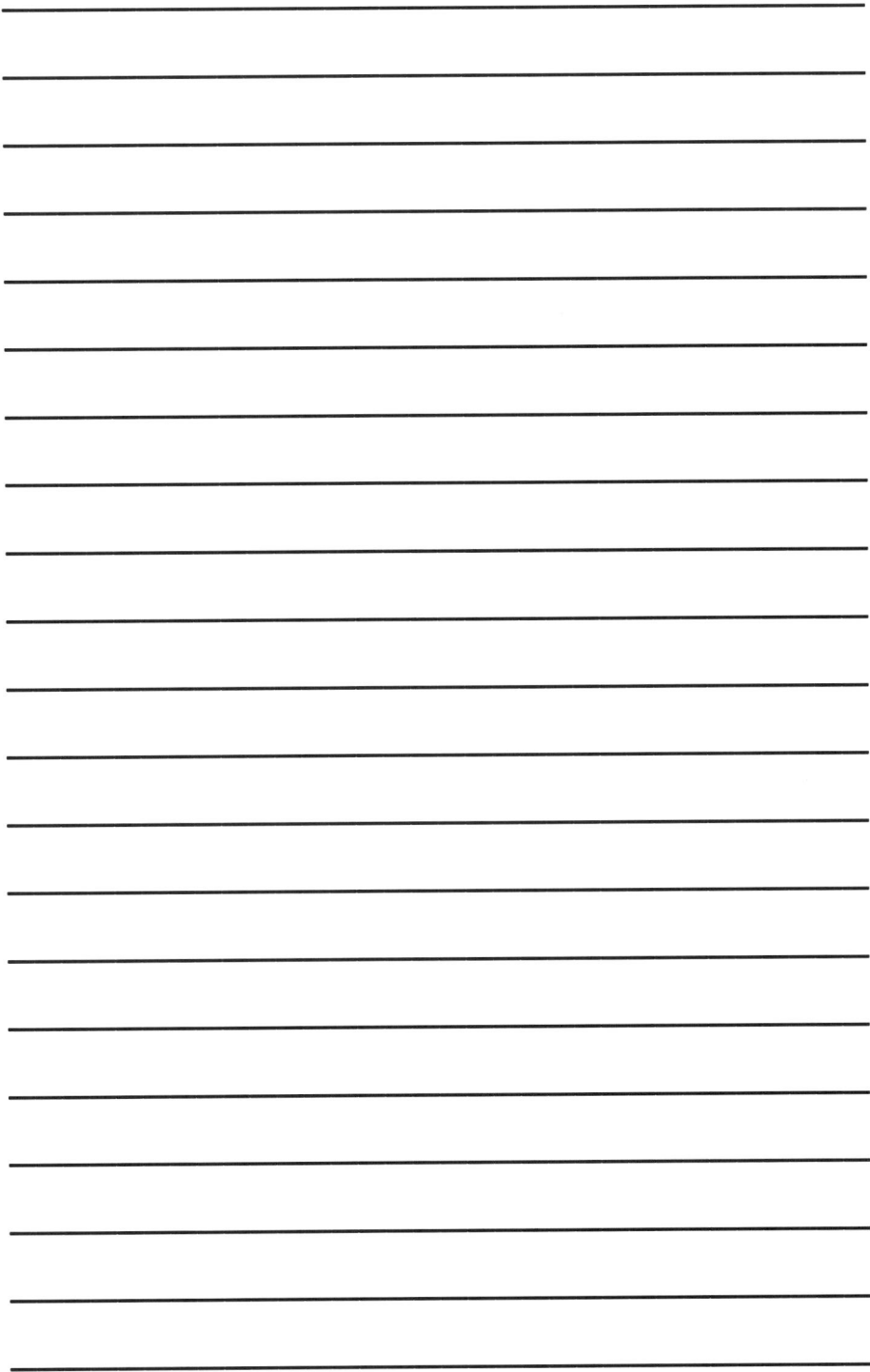

Word:

But seek first the kingdom of God and his righteousness, and all these things will be added to you. Matthew 6:33

Prayer:

Father – I want to seek you – and only you – even during my struggles. Help me Lord – help me to remember that when I focus my eyes on you everything else comes into clearer focus. May I see those around me as you see them. I want to give grace and be love. I love you. Amen.

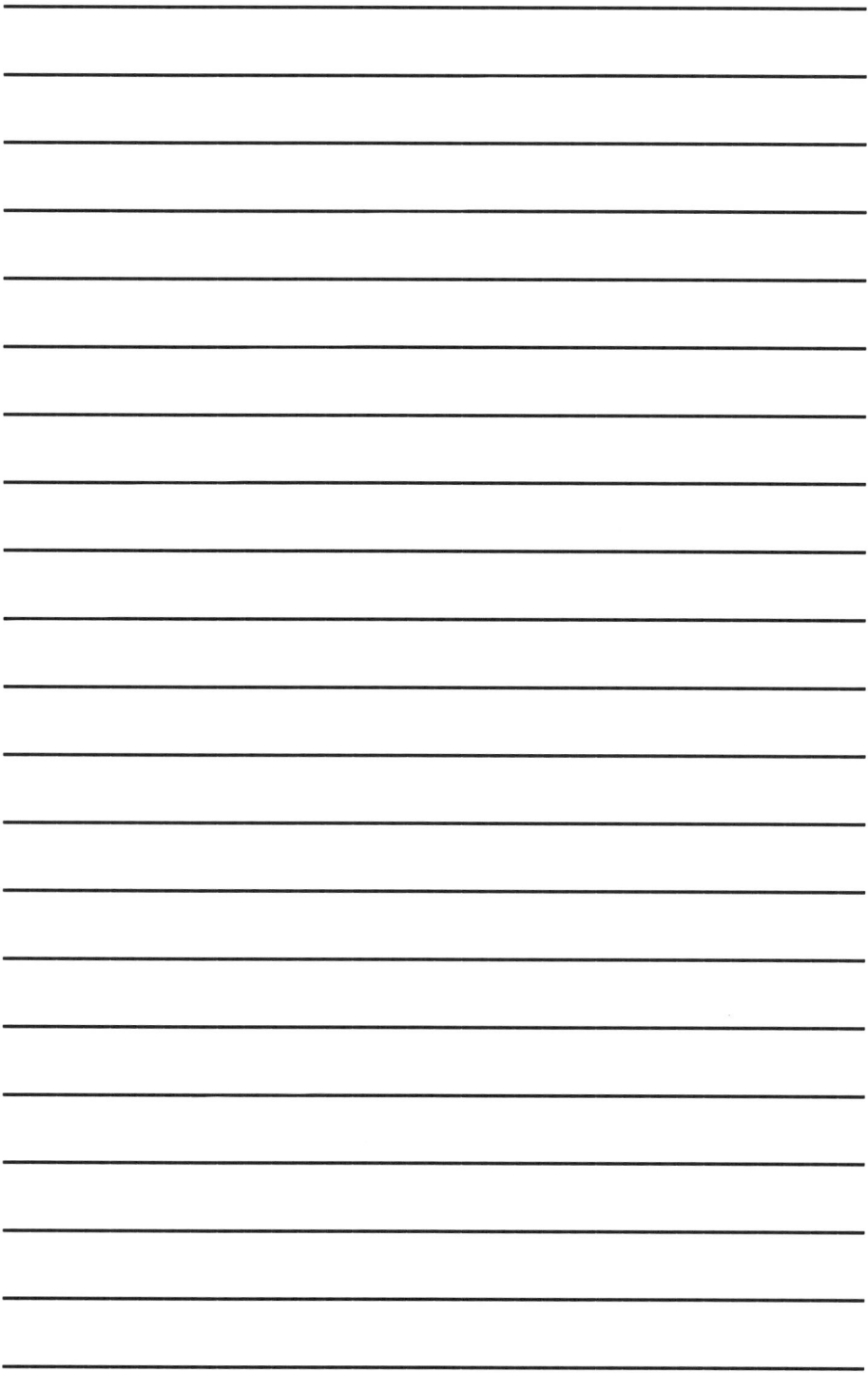

Word:

I can do all things through him who strengthens me. Philippians 4:13

Prayer:

Lord – this scripture has helped me so many times. It rolls off my tongue during difficult times but today I want to etch this scripture on my heart in a way that allows me to really live my life in a way that reflects that I believe it. Knowing I can do all things and actually "doing all things" through you are different. Give me boldness to walk in your love and light. The world can hurt, but your word can heal. Amen.

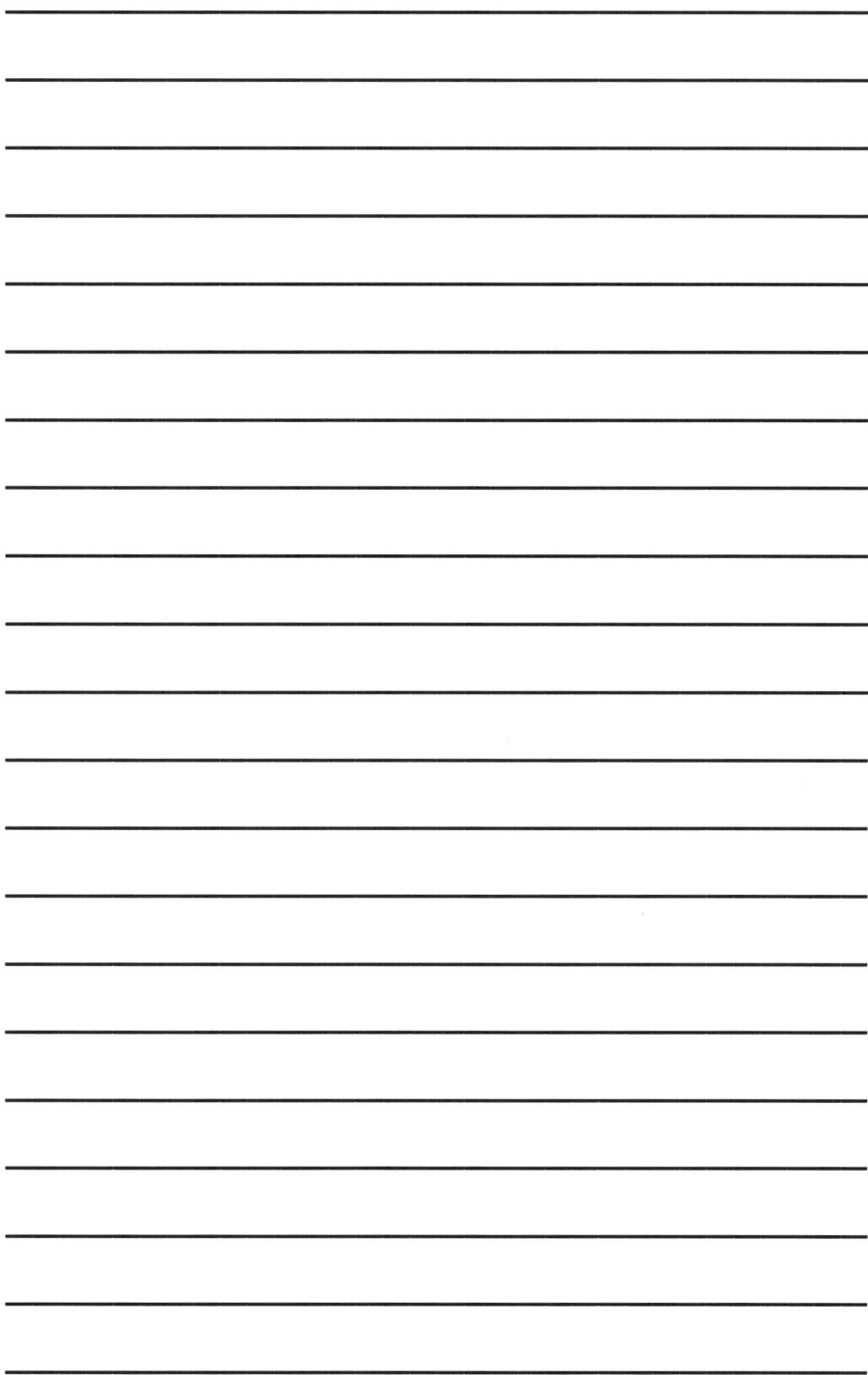

Word:
He has made everything beautiful in its time. Also, he has put eternity into man's heart, yet so that he cannot find out what God has done from the beginning to the end. Ecclesiastes 3:11

Prayer:
Daddy – thank you for this promise. My past hurts. My present is scary, but I know my future is secure because of this promise. I believe that you will make all things beautiful. Everything will be made beautiful in its time. I want to wait on you Lord. Amen.

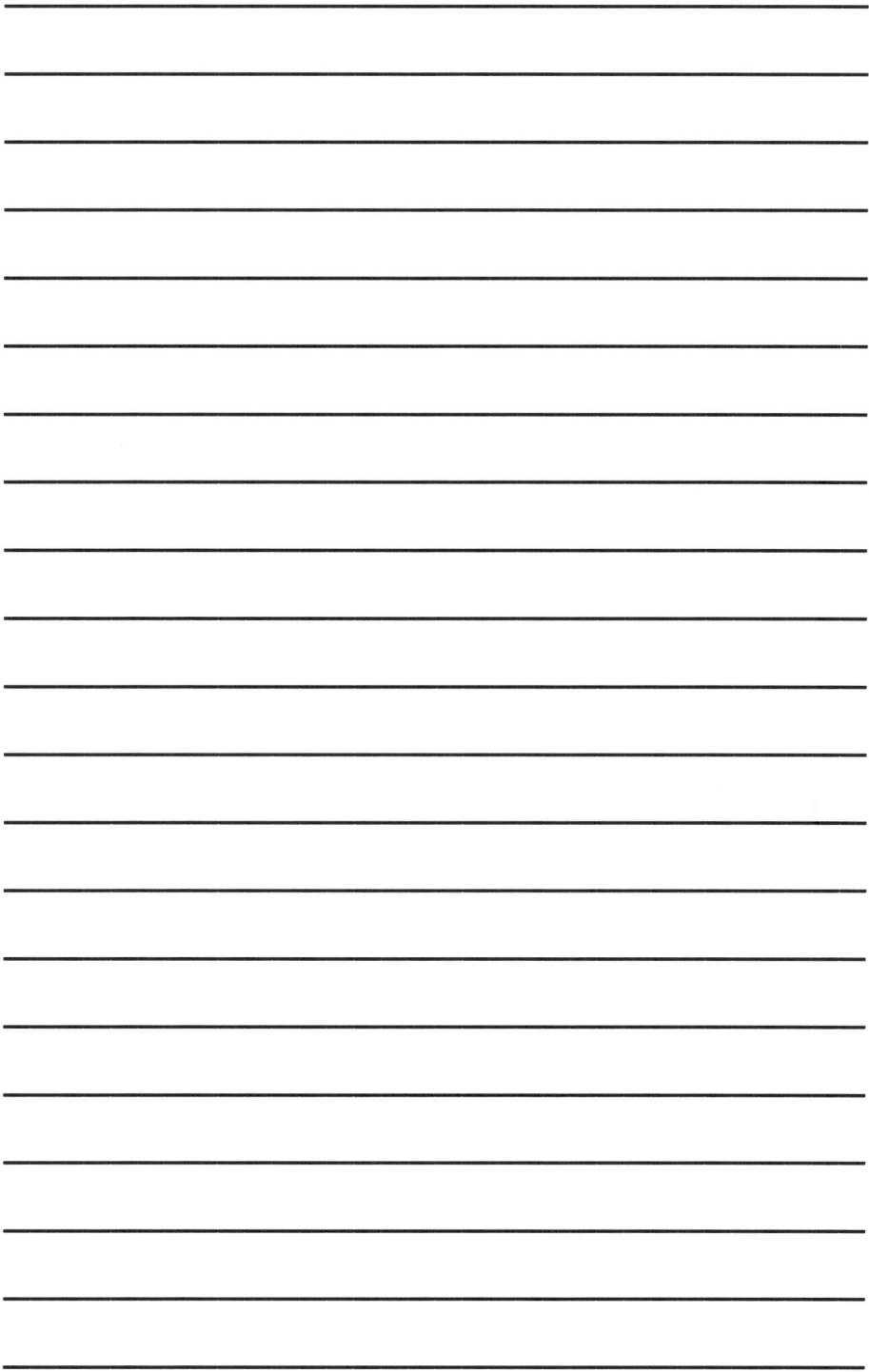

Word:

Do not be anxious about anything, but in everything by prayer and supplication with thanksgiving let your requests be made known to God. Philippians 4:6

Prayer:

Father – Really? Is this possible? I want to believe that it is. Please give me the peace and comfort to rest in you and to not be anxious about anything. The hurts of my life have made me anxious but really do want to live out this scripture. I cry out to you today and know you hear me. I love you. Amen.

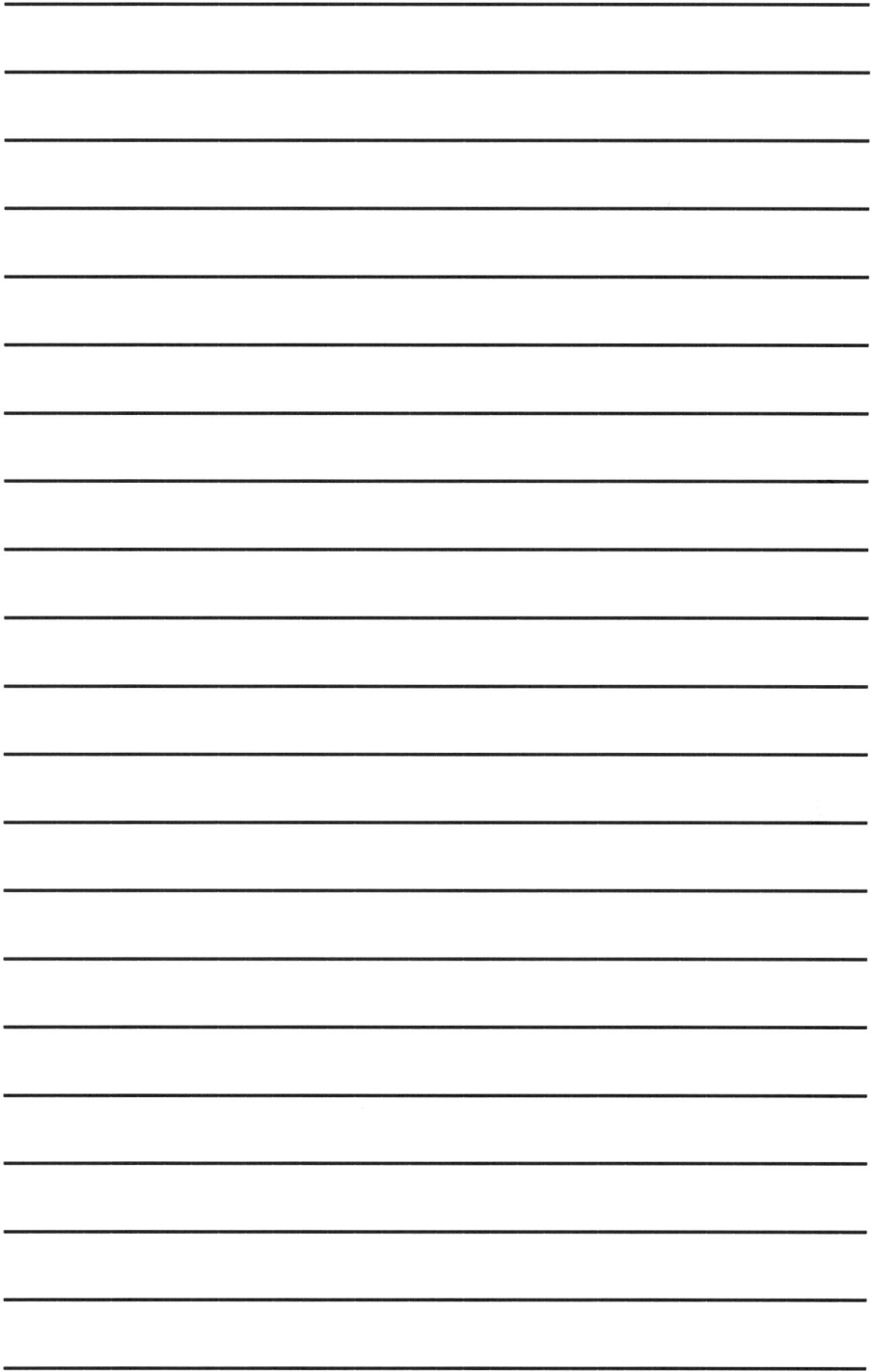

Word:

Trust in the Lord with all your heart, and do not lean on your own understanding. In all your ways acknowledge him, and he will make straight your paths. Proverbs 3:5-6

Prayer:

Almighty God – I call you Father, Lord, Abba, Papa and Daddy but today I want to remember that you are the Almighty God and I can trust you to lead me. Your ways are always better than my ways – I pray that today and always I remember that. Lord thank you so much for hearing my prayers. Draw me close to you. I love you. Amen.

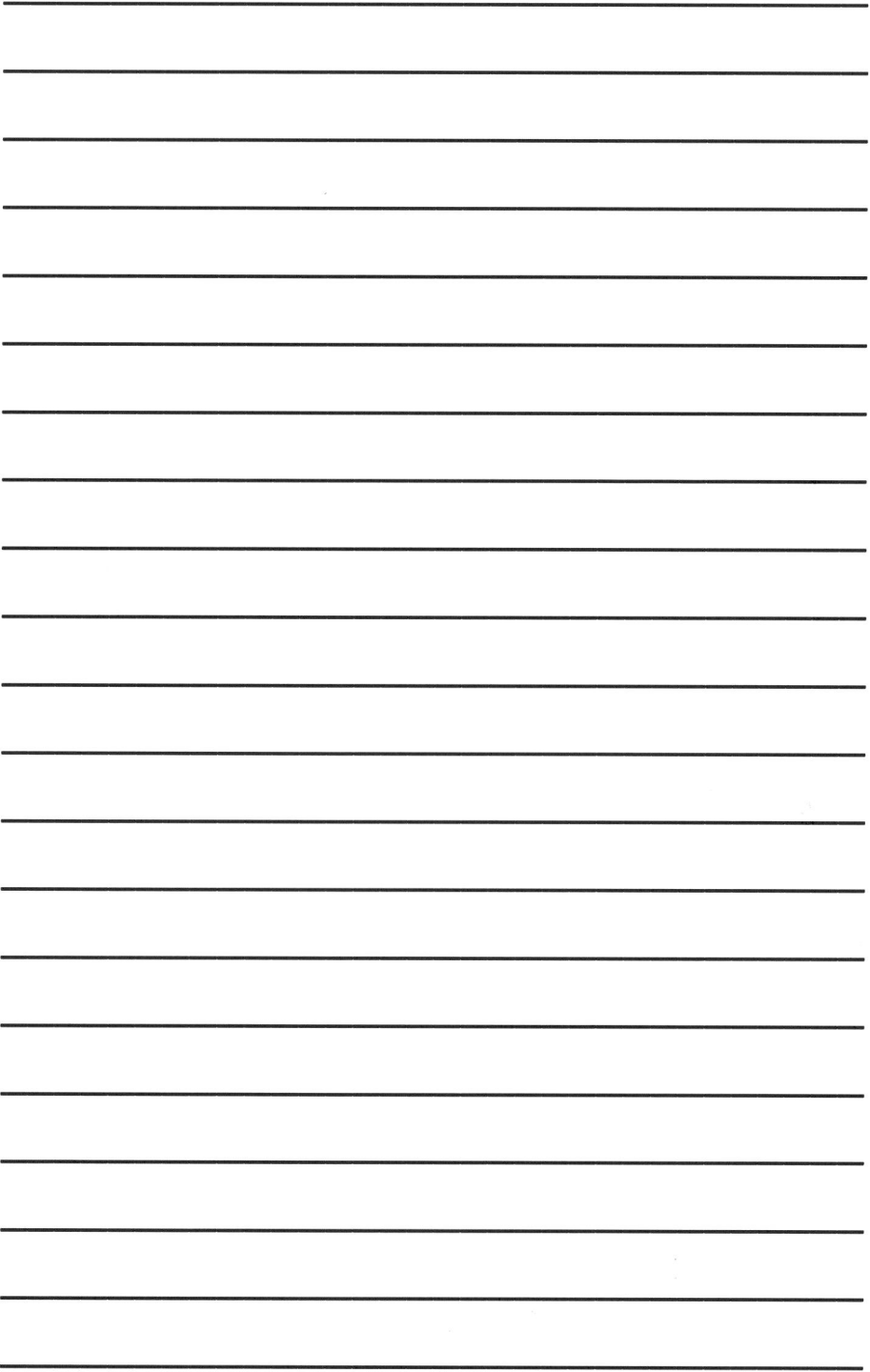

Word:

It is good for me that I was afflicted, that I might learn your statutes. The law of your mouth is better to me than thousands of gold and silver pieces. Psalm 119:71-72

Prayer:

Father – I never thought my afflictions would be a good thing but I have learned that during my struggles I lean on you more. Following what you have for me truly is better than anything I could do on my own. Help me make choices that reflect the fact that I know I am loved by you even on my bad days. I love you. Amen.

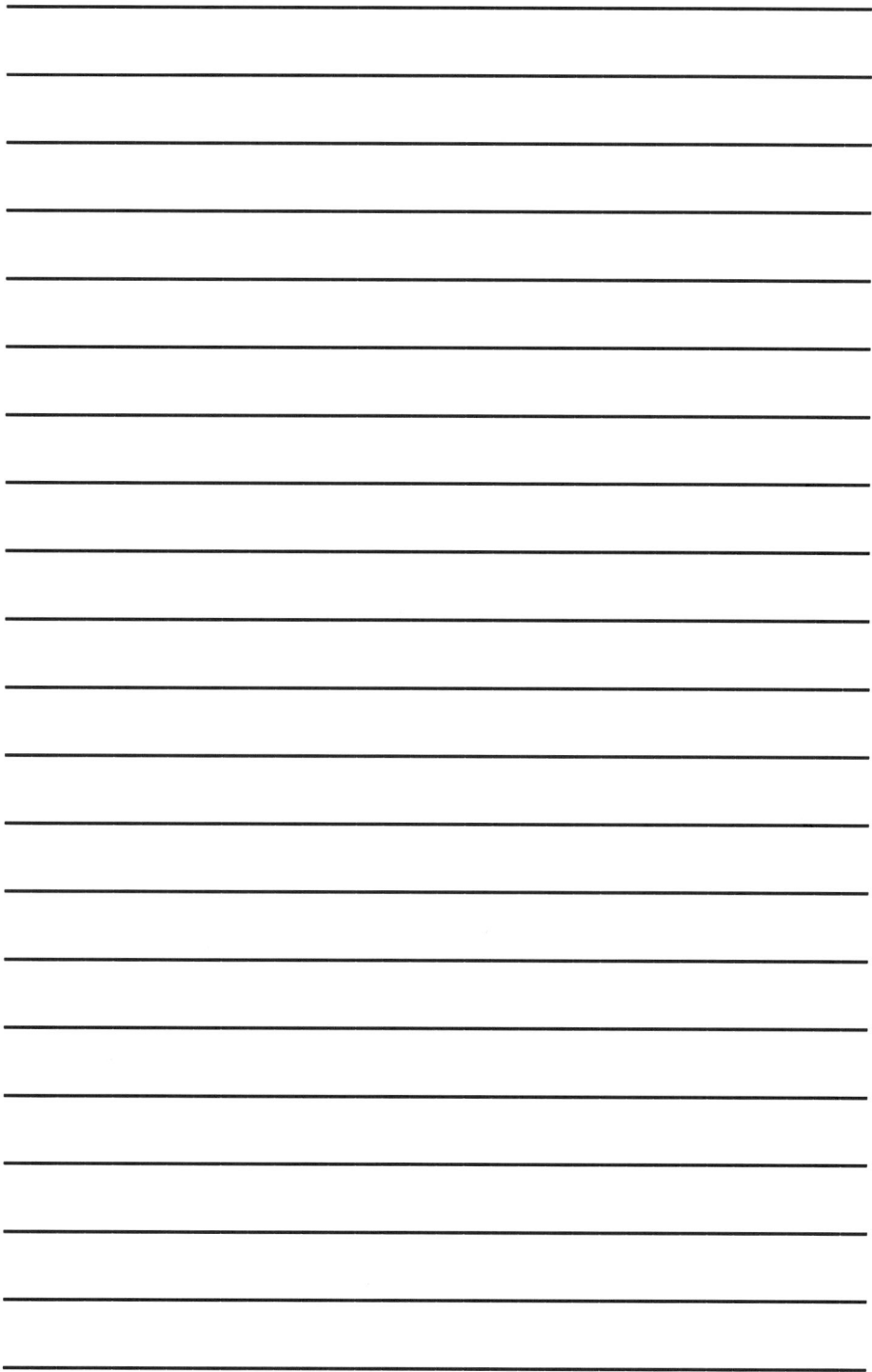

Word:

I praise you, for I am fearfully and wonderfully made. Wonderful are your works; my soul knows it very well. Psalm 139:14

Prayer:

Papa – what a blessing to know that you made me exactly as I am. The hurts that I have experienced have made me forget who I am and who I belong to. Today I pray that I can focus on the truth of who I am – which is yours. Thank you for making me exactly as you have made me – struggles and all because I know you will get all the glory for my life. I love you. Amen.

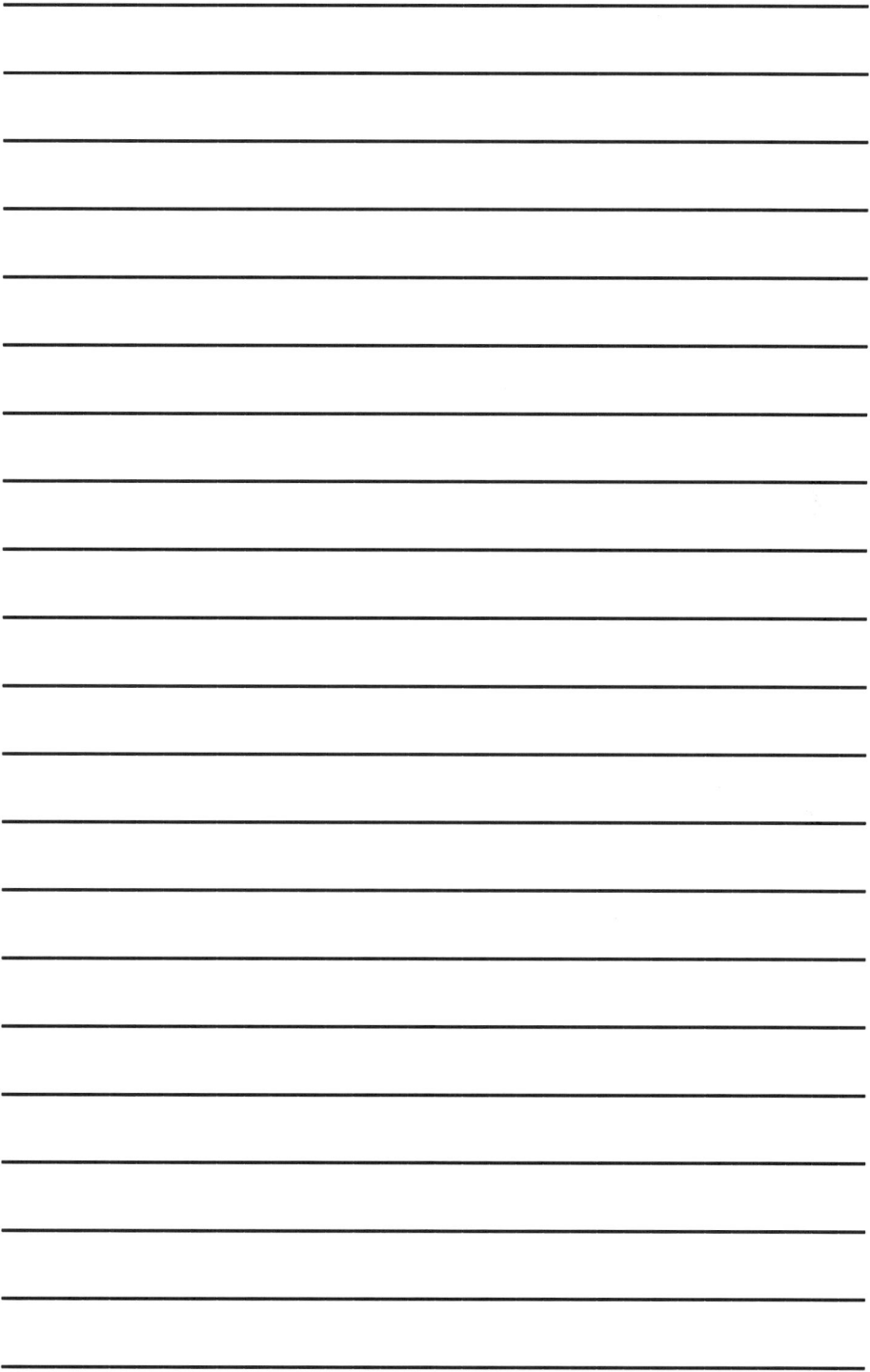

Word:

You shall love the Lord your God with all your heart and with all your soul and with all your mind. This is the great and first commandment. And a second is like it: You shall love your neighbor as yourself. On these two commandments depend all the Law and the Prophets.
Matthew 22:37-40

Prayer:

Father – this is everything. Please help me remember that to love you and others well I must love myself too. I give you my heart, soul and mind. Help me give grace and be love. I love you. Amen.

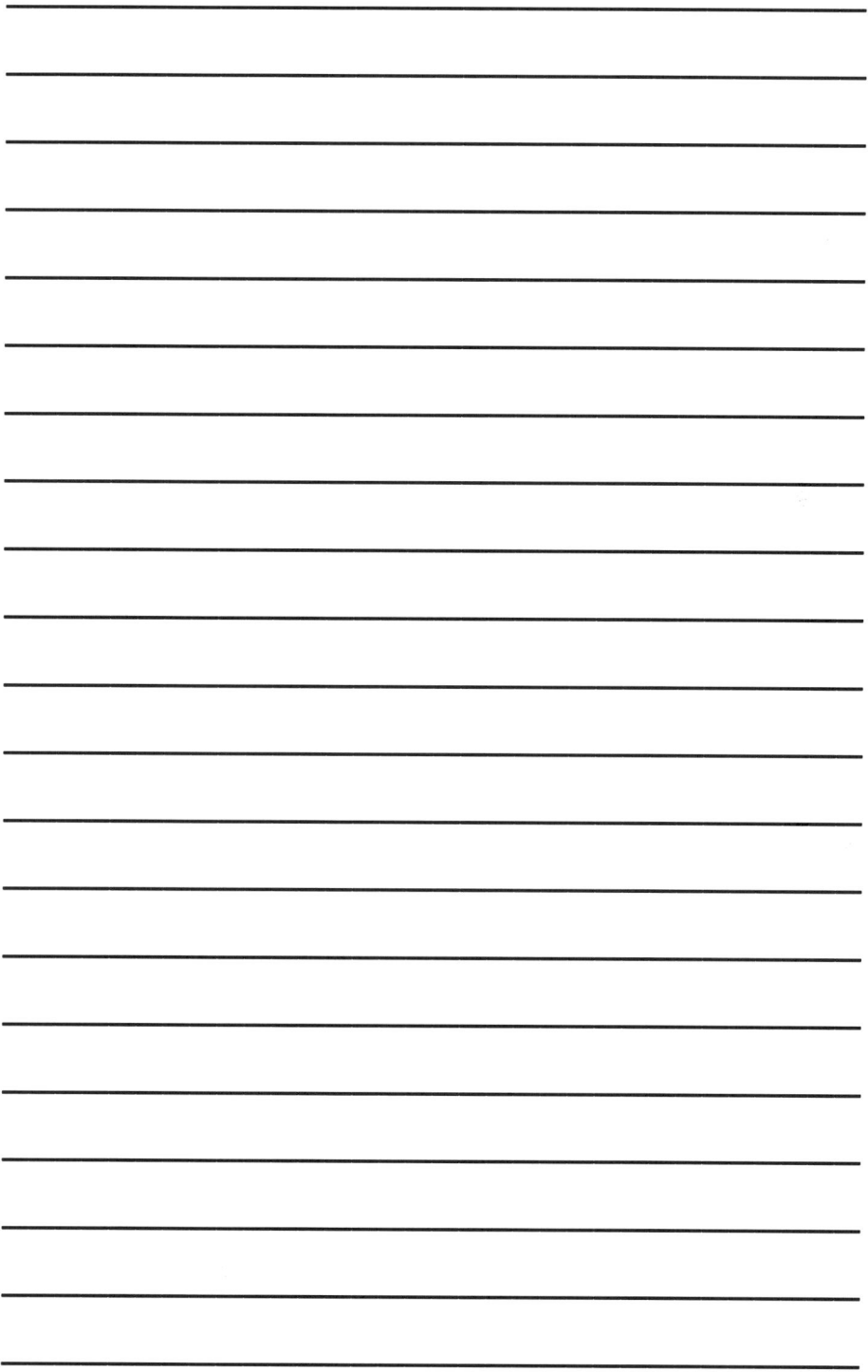

Word:

So now faith, hope, and love abide, these three; but the greatest of these is love. 1 Corinthians 13:13

Prayer:

Daddy – you are love so it makes sense that the greatest of these is love. I open my heart to receive your love. I want to shine your light to all the world and let them see your glory in all that you do through my life. Heal me Lord from the inside out and fill me with your love, completely. I love you more than words can explain. Amen.

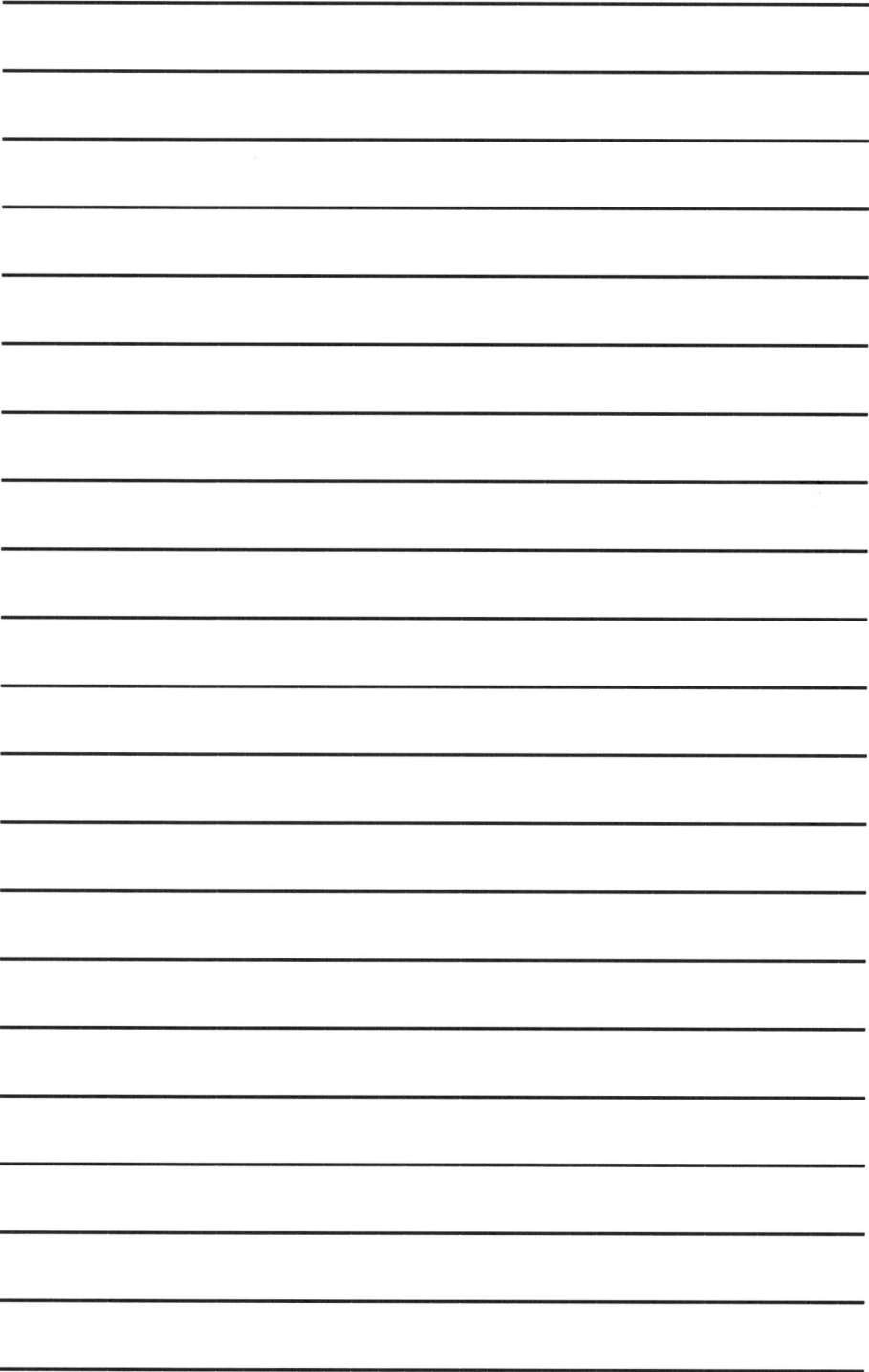

Word:

The Lord is my strength and my shield; in him my heart trusts, and I am helped; my heart exults, and with my song I give thanks to him.
Psalm 28:7

Prayer:

Father – I claim this today. Be my strength. My shield. Protect me. I trust you with my life. My past hurts are just that. Past. I am focused on living my life today in your truth and grace. I pray these words over my life today. I give you thanks for everything you have done for me and will do for me in the future. I am blessed to be your child. Amen.

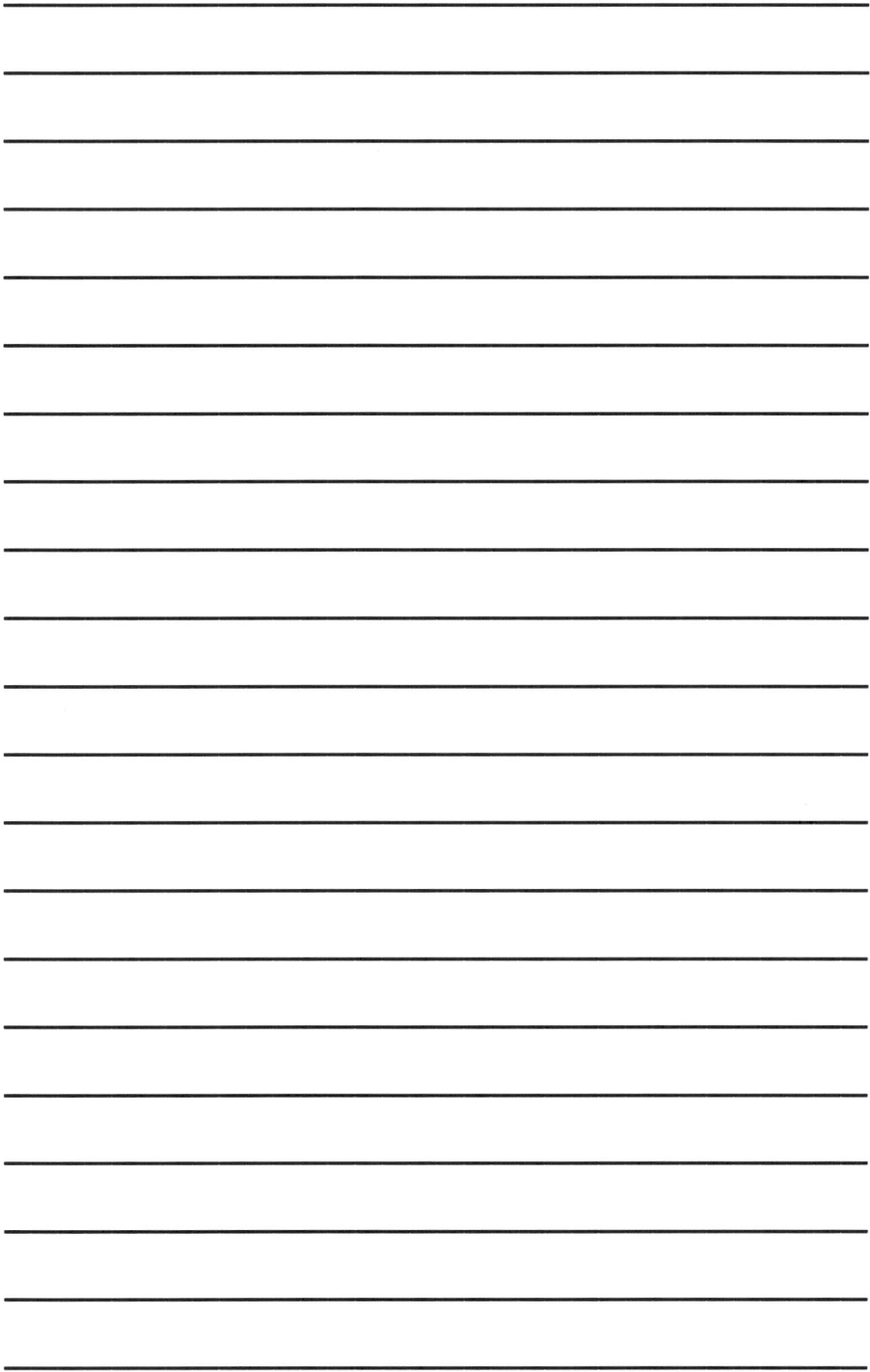

Word:

The Lord is near to the brokenhearted and saves the crushed in spirit. Psalm 34:18

Prayer:

Abba Father – some days I don't feel like you are near to me and then I read your word and am reminded that you are near to the brokenhearted. My heart is healing but surely was broken. Thank you for allowing my heart to heal and to still be open to giving and receiving love. I want to be close to you and walk in your ways. Guide my steps, Lord. I love you today and forever. Amen.

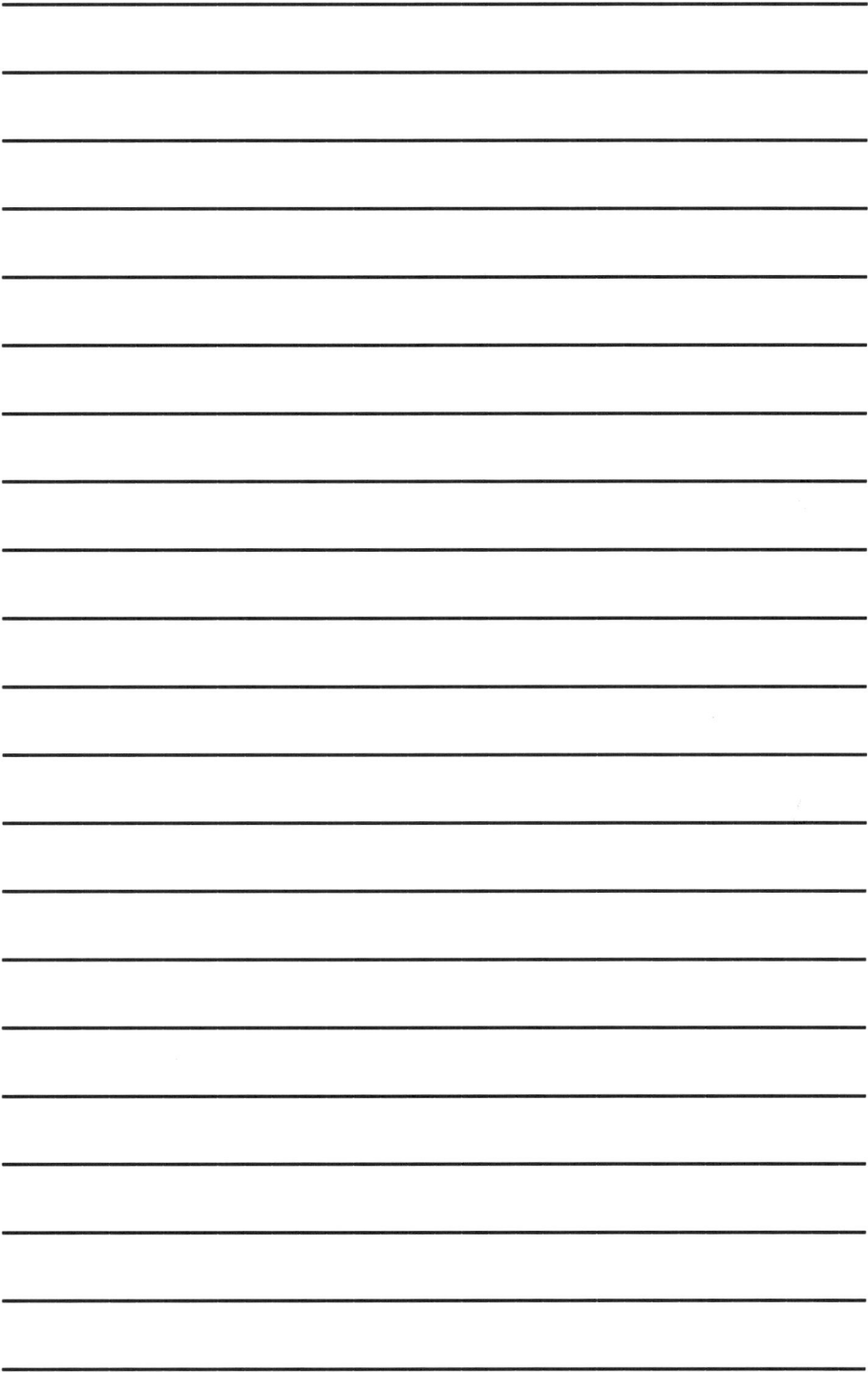

Word:

As it is my eager expectation and hope that I will not be at all ashamed, but that with full courage now as always Christ will be honored in my body, whether by life or by death. Philippians 1:20

Prayer:

Father – may my life always be a reflection of the love and grace you have given me. I want to honor you in all I do. I have made so many mistakes and bad choices in the past but want to lean on you today and every day to have the strength to walk in the truth of your love. Faithfully Yours. Amen.

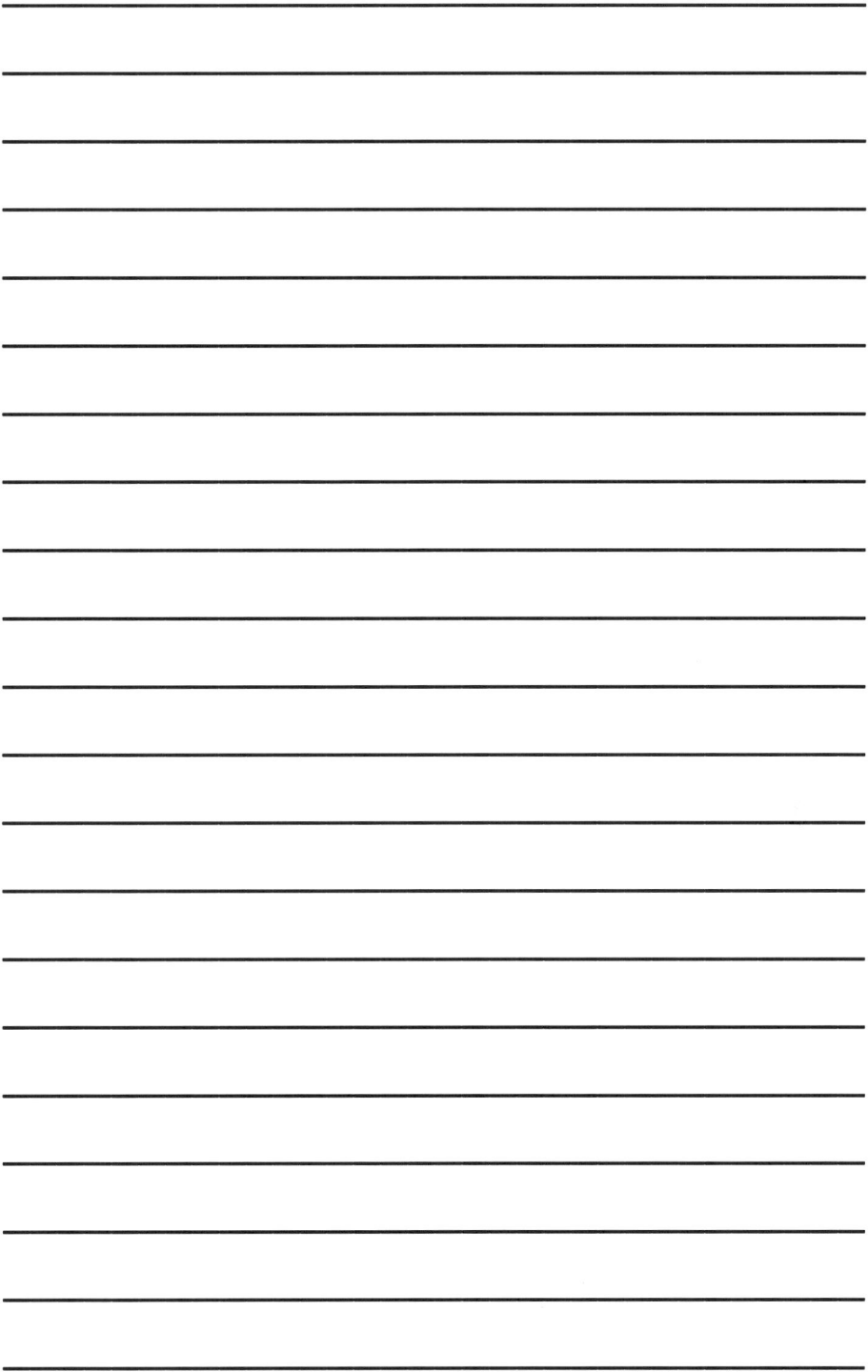

Word:

For God alone my soul waits in silence; from him comes my salvation. He alone is my rock and my salvation, my fortress; I shall not be greatly shaken. Psalm 62:1-2

Prayer:

Daddy – you know – silence. It hasn't been my strength. I am "wordy" and find silence awkward sometimes. You are my Lord and I have my salvation in only you. If I need to be quiet – let me be quiet. If I need to speak up – let me speak up. May everything I do bring you glory and honor. I love you. Amen.

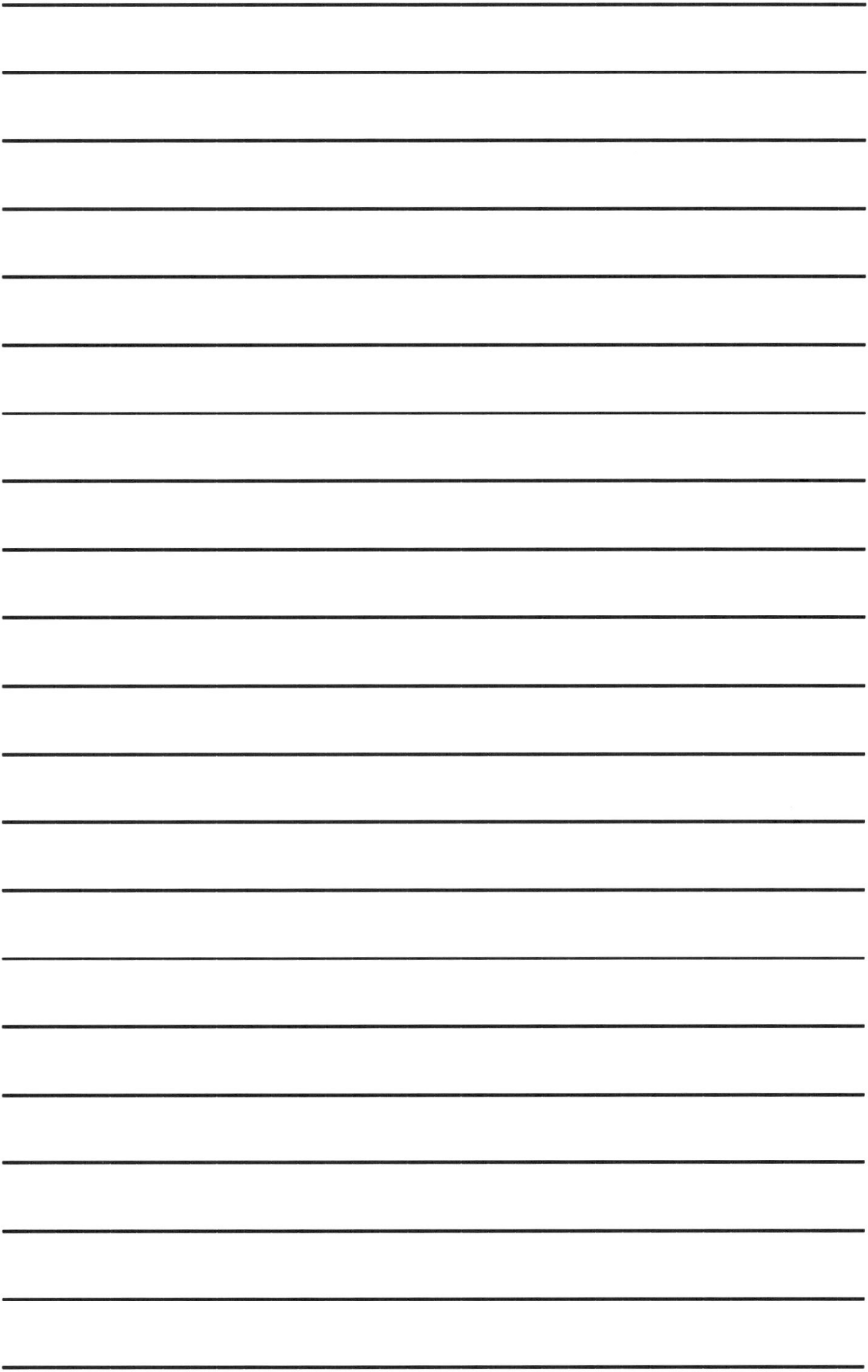

Word:

He who dwells in the shelter of the Most High will abide in the shadow of the Almighty. Psalm 91:1

Prayer:

Abba – this scripture has meant so much to me. Even on the bad days – when I didn't know if I would make it – I knew this scripture was true. I will dwell with you all my days. I am safe with you. Thank you for being my protector and covering me in your shadow. Thank you for not letting the darkness overtake me. I trust you. Always yours. Amen.

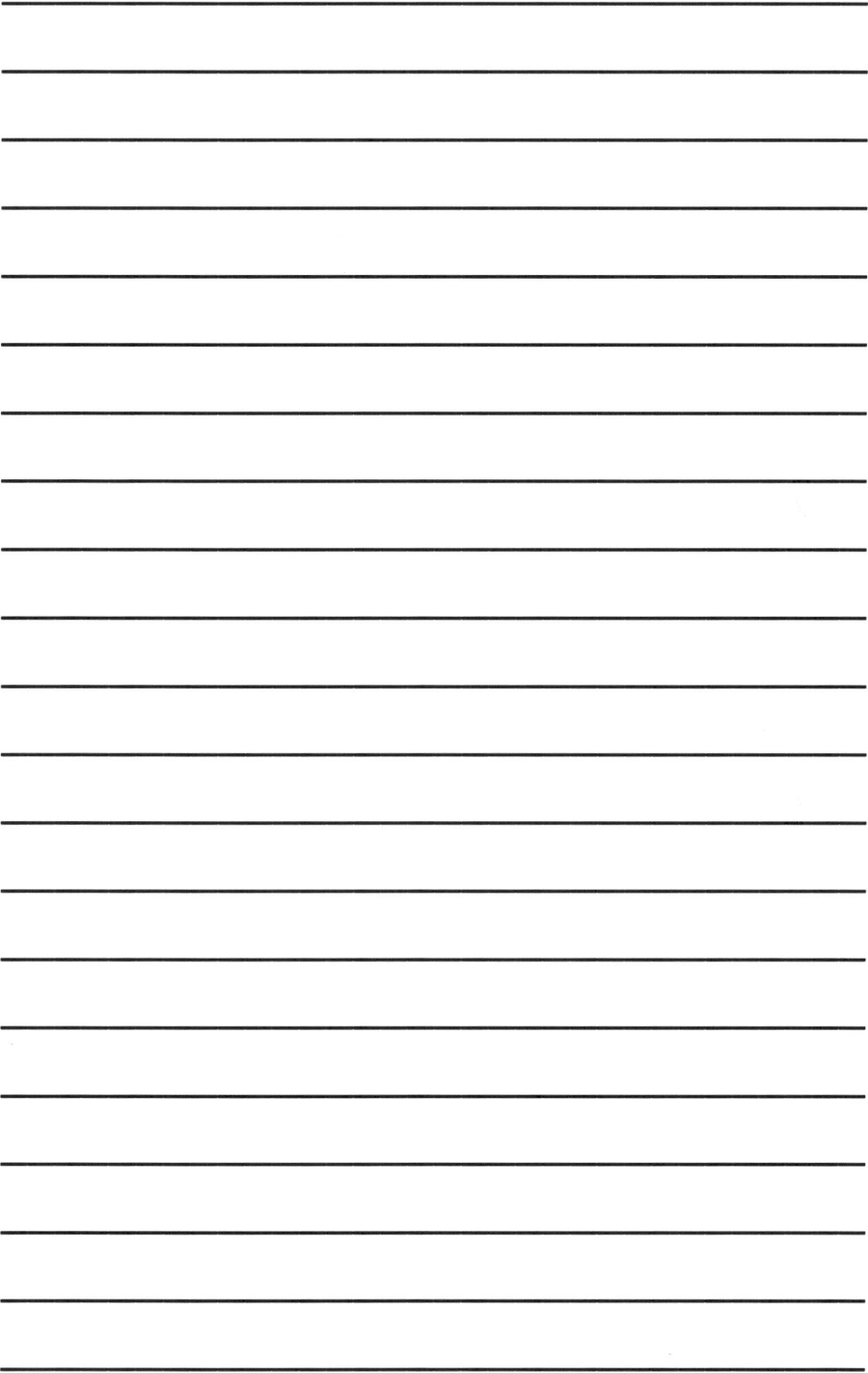

Word:

Mightier than the thunders of many waters, mightier than the waves of the sea, the Lord on high is mighty!
Psalm 93:4

Prayer:

Papa – You are amazing. Full of power. Full of love. Full of grace. You are mighty and worthy of praise. I am in awe of you. Thank you for loving me. Thank you for healing my wounds and helping me create a life filled with love, mercy and grace. In the middle of the storms of my life, I pray that I remember that you are the mighty God who has my life in the palm of his hand. I love you. Amen.

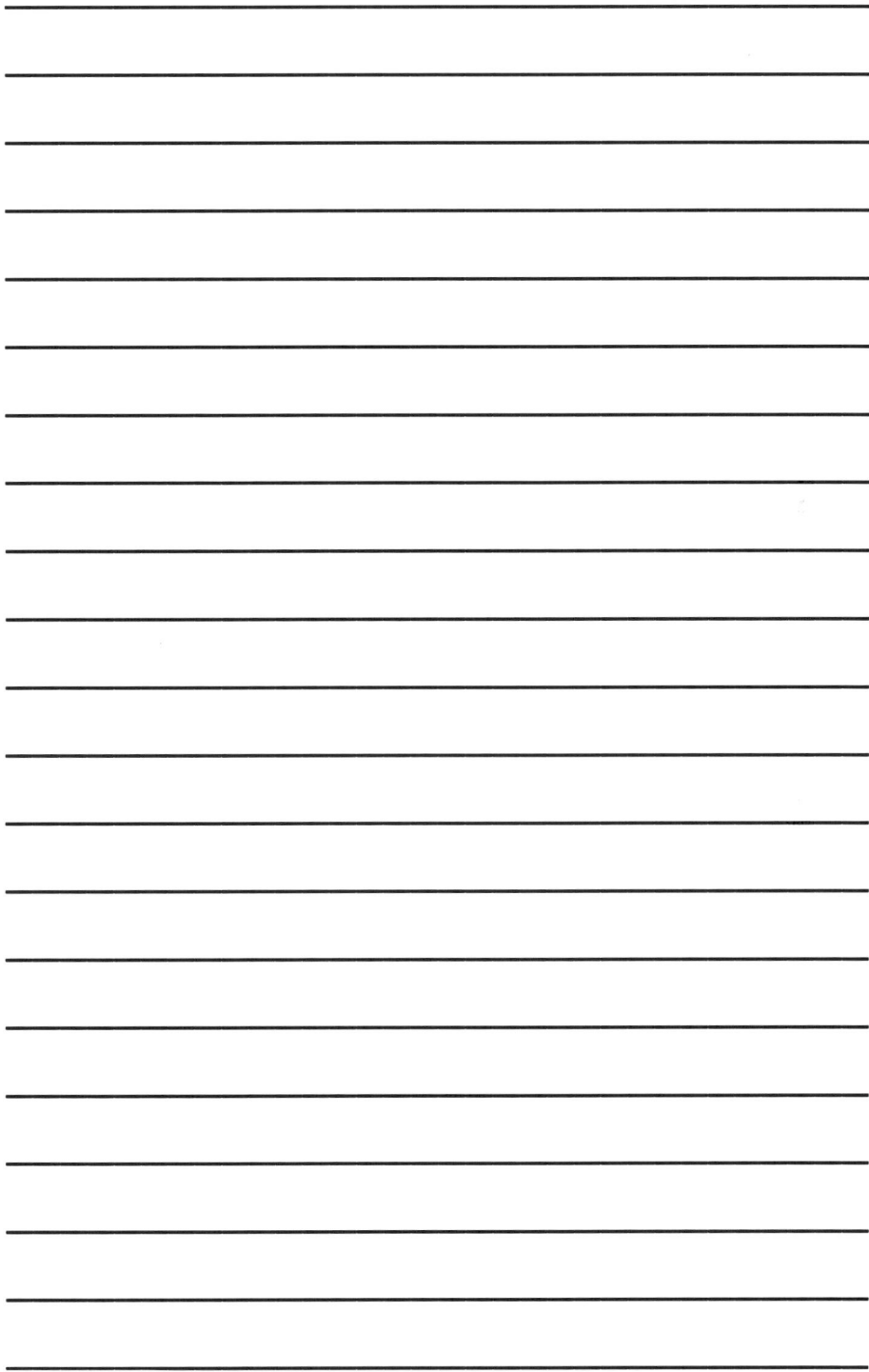

Word:

But I call to God, and the Lord will save me. Evening and morning and at noon I utter my complaint and moan, and he hears my voice. He redeems my soul in safety from the battle that I wage, for many are arrayed against me. God will give ear and humble them, he who is enthroned from of old, Selah because they do not change and do not fear God. Psalm 55:16-19

Prayer:

Father – You see my wounds and have heard my prayers. Thank you for hearing me. I love you dearly. Amen.

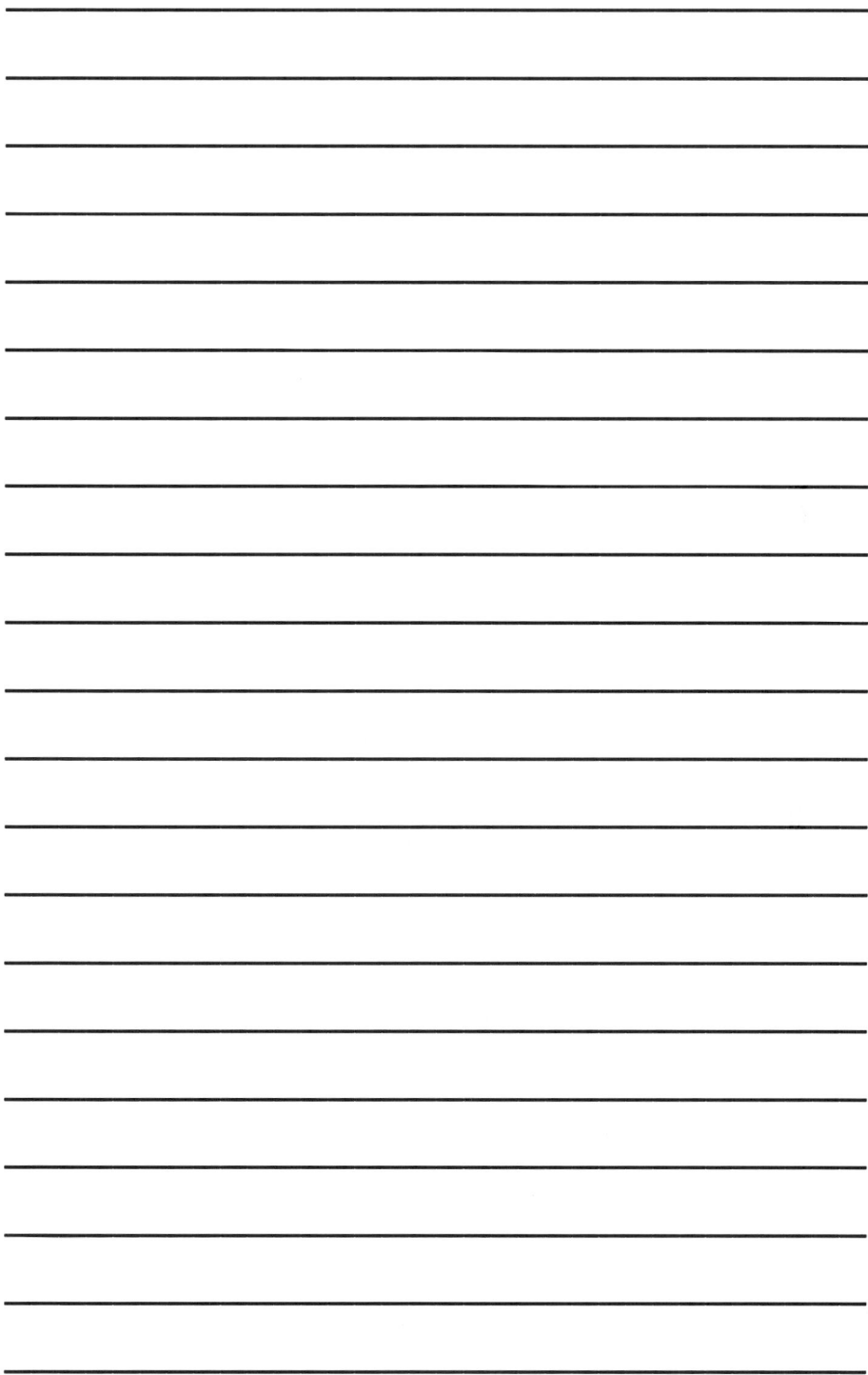

Word:

But God shows his love for us in that while we were still sinners, Christ died for us. Romans 5:8

Prayer:

Creator of everything – that is who you are. It is amazing that the grace covered cross paid for all my sins. Even while I was still a sinner you sent your son to die for me. It is scandalous, to say the least. Because of what you did for me I know that I can face any challenge that comes my way. I accept your love. And am in complete awe of all you have done for me. I am yours. Amen.

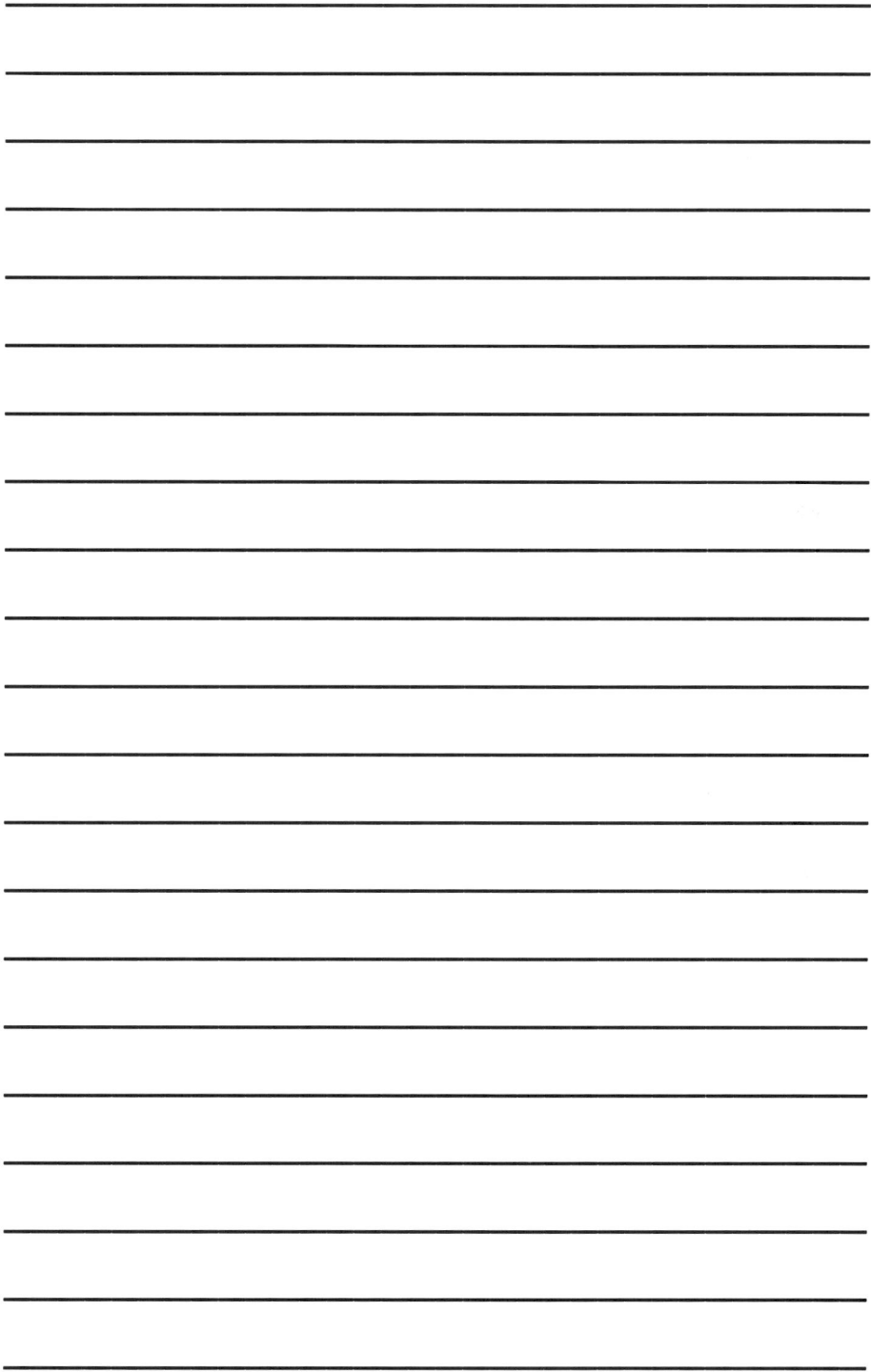

Word:

The word of the LORD came to Jeremiah: "Behold, I am the LORD, the God of all flesh. Is anything too hard for me? Jeremiah 32:26-27

Prayer:

Father – NOTHING is too hard for you. I believe that you want what is best for me. I believe that when I give you my hurts and struggles you can heal them, but I also realize that sometimes you don't change my circumstances because you want to change my heart. I give you my heart and my life. Thank you for being the healer of my soul. I love you. Amen.

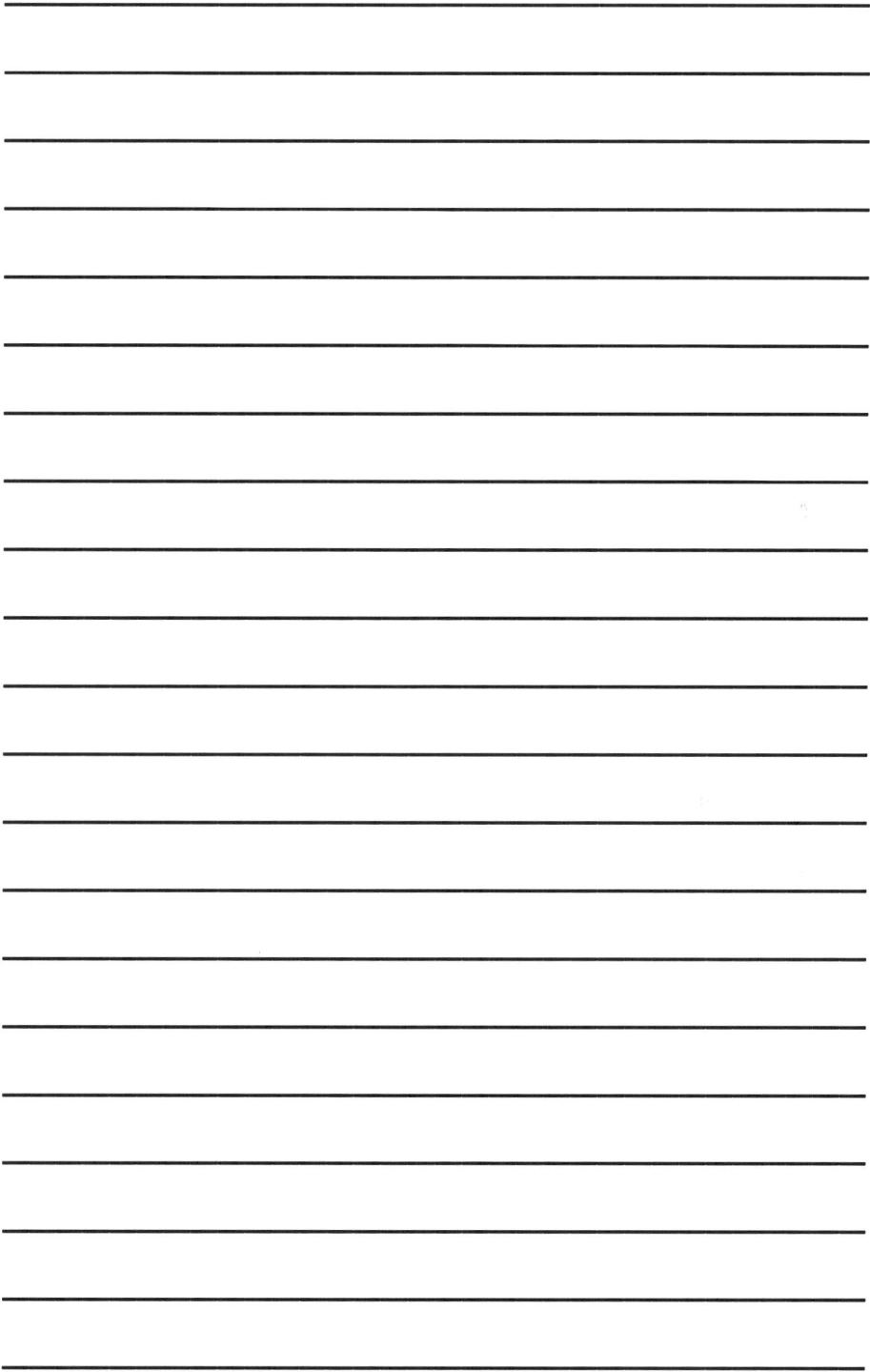

Word:

Count it all joy, my brothers, when you meet trials of various kinds, for you know that the testing of your faith produces steadfastness. And let steadfastness have its full effect, that you may be perfect and complete, lacking in nothing. If any of you lacks wisdom, let him ask God, who gives generously to all without reproach, and it will be given him. James 1:2-5

Prayer:

Daddy – Trials – that is something I am familiar with. Please let me find the joy in everything. Especially the trials. I am yours. Amen.

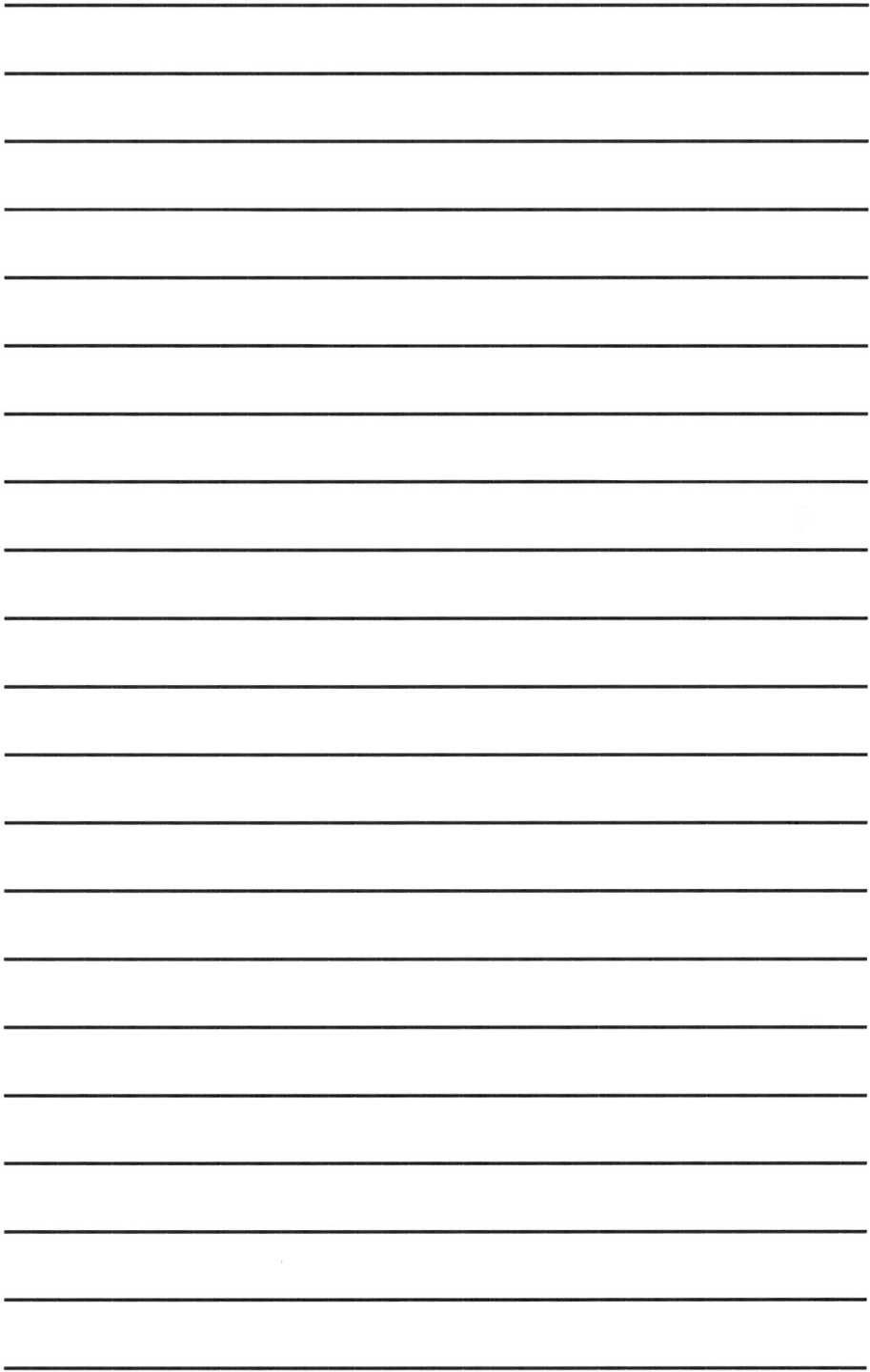

Word:

When you pass through the waters, I will be with you; and through the rivers, they shall not overwhelm you; when you walk through fire you shall not be burned, and the flame shall not consume you. Isaiah 43:2

Prayer:

Almighty God – thank you for being with me during my struggles. Thank you for not allowing those issues to completely consume me. Thank you for the continued healing I am experiencing through your grace and love. Thank you for redeeming me and making me new. You are my everything. Amen.

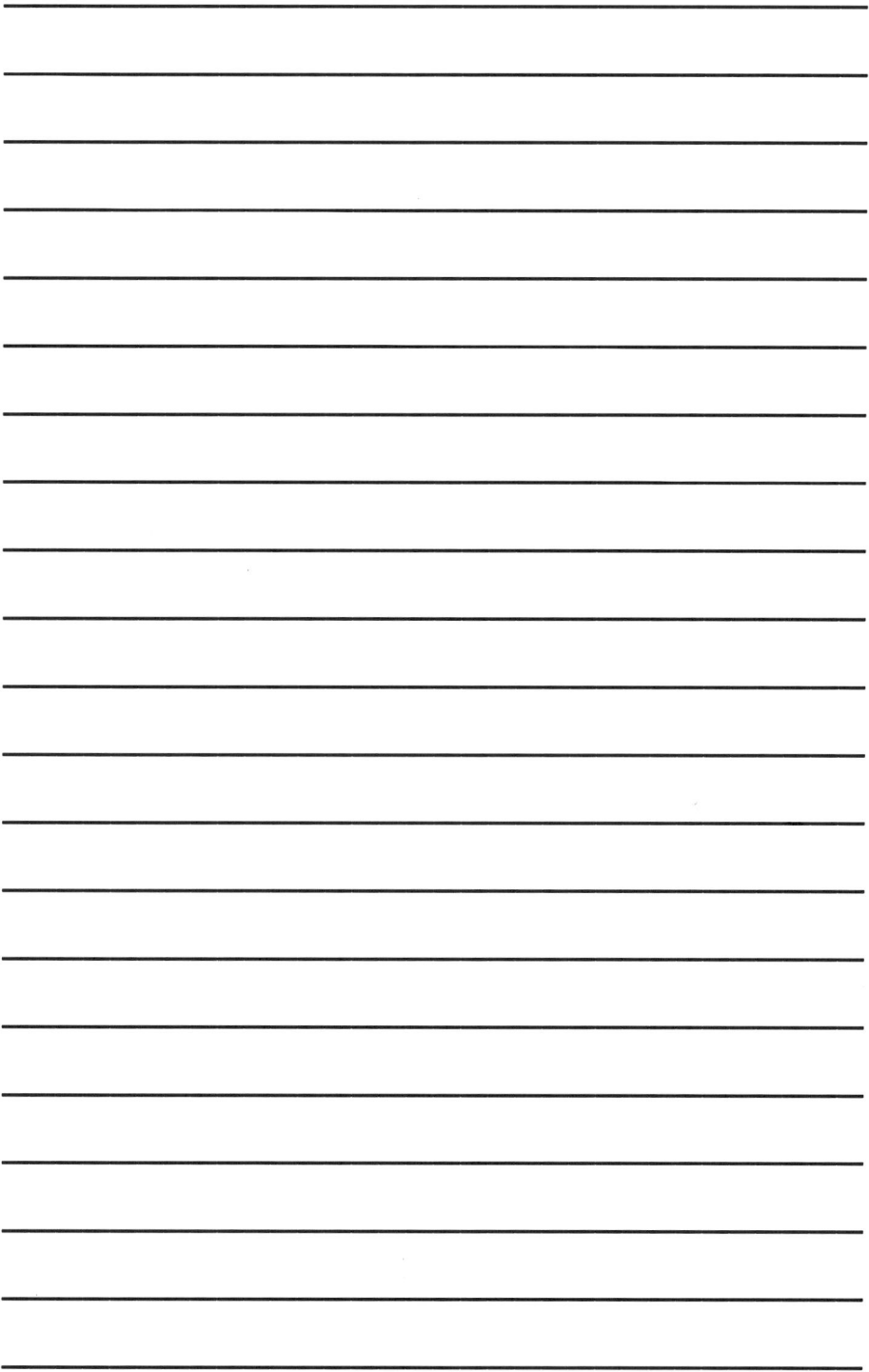

Word:
Wait for the Lord; be strong, and let your heart take courage; wait for the Lord! Psalm 27:14

Prayer:
Lord – I will wait for you and be strong. I will take courage and wait for you. Waiting is a challenge, or it has been in the past. Give my eyes the ability to see when I need to wait and when you are telling me to move. May my life be completely in step with what you have for me. Allow me to heal in a way that will allow for others to know that you are God and able to do anything. I love you. Amen.

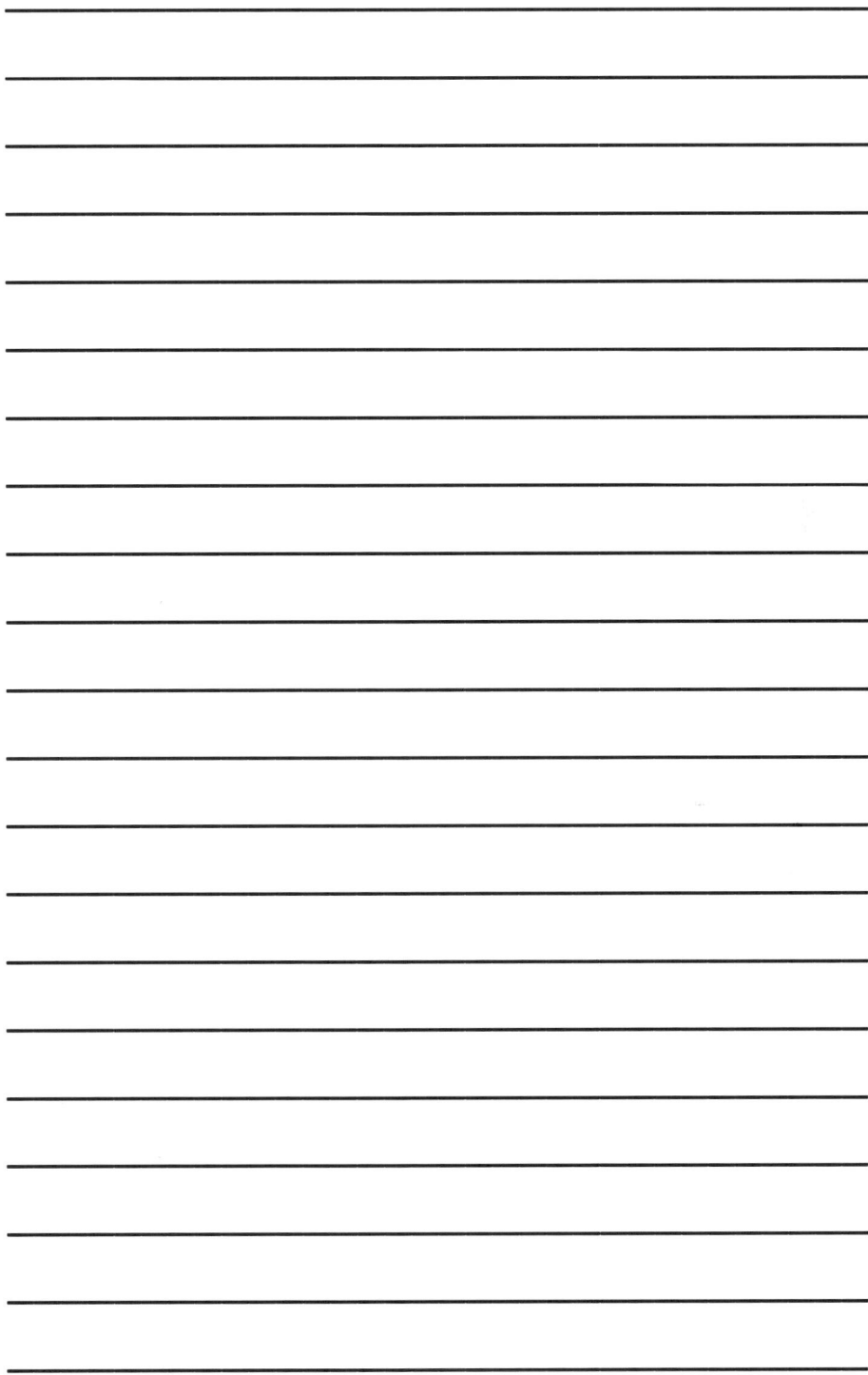

Word:
It is the Lord who goes before you. He will be with you; he will not leave you or forsake you. Do not fear or be dismayed. Deuteronomy 31:8

Prayer:
Father – I love how you tell us the same thing in a different way throughout the Bible. You have told me many times that you will never leave or forsake me. Thank you for loving me. Thank you for never leaving me. Be with me today to help me trust you more and more every day. I love you. Amen.

80038282R00049

Made in the USA
San Bernardino, CA
21 June 2018